4 & Divorced

# 24 & Divorced

From Tragedy to Triumph

Leonardo Cavalli

| Library of Congress Control Number: | | 2015905213 |
|---|---|---|
| ISBN: | Hardcover | 978-1-5035-4260-0 |
| | Softcover | 978-1-5035-4261-7 |
| | eBook | 978-1-5035-4262-4 |

Print information available on the last page.

Rev. date: 05/14/2015

**To order additional copies of this book, contact:**
Xlibris
1-888-795-4274
www.Xlibris.com
Orders@Xlibris.com
703848

# CONTENTS

# MY CURRENT CHAOS

Hello friends,

My name is Leonardo Cavalli, and I was twenty-four when I got divorced. Right now, I am currently twenty-five years old, writing this from inside a medical research facility in Chicago. I am in this research facility because—to put it frankly—I'm homeless, broke on the outside, and a wreck on the inside. I'm scared of my past, miserable in my present state and unsure about my future. For the first time in my life, I'm not a hundred percent sure what I believe in anymore. However, one thing I am sure of is that an individual can either make money from drugs and sex, or drugs and science. Today I've chosen drugs and science.

I just signed into this medical research facility. I'm looking around because I have never been in a place like this. The only time I've ever even heard of places like this are in horror films, right before things go horribly wrong in a freak accident. I wish I could tell you exactly what this research drug these doctors are about to give me does, but to be completely honest, I don't really care right now. All I know is that it's a thirty-nine-day-straight locked-down study where they will give me a check for ten thousand dollars if I can make it through to the end. I hate needles, and they will have to give me well over one hundred of them throughout the time I'm here. This is now the only option I have for a chance to get my old life back, and I'm going to take it. I don't remember all the side effects that the doctors warned me about, but I do remember one of them being blindness. Ironically, at this point in life there is nothing worth seeing anyway; so I feel that I have got nothing to lose. I mean, I'm about to "celebrate" my twenty-sixth birthday while I'm still locked up in this research facility.

The first procedure is about to take place, where the nurses are about to give me my first needle and doses. I'm afraid. I'm honestly so afraid right now. The nurse asks me if I'm okay, so I fake a smile and nod as if to say yes. She asks me which arm I want to get the needle in, and I say, "I think the veins are better in my left one." Past experiences taught me that. Anxiety takes over as millions of questions start racing through my head, and then it begins.

Me: [In my head] *Am I doing the right thing? Am I really about to go through with this?*

Nurse pulls my arm toward her and tells me to relax.

Me: *What if these needles and drugs they give me destroy my mind and creativity altogether . . . and forever? What if I become mentally retarded.*

Nurse proceeds to strap my arm down.

Me: *What if I actually do go blind?*

Nurse taps my forearm, waiting for my veins to rise.

Me: What if I can't have children after this? *What if I really do die from this?*

Nurse: "Oh, I found a good one."

Me: *I never got to tell my parents how sorry I was for all the pain I caused them these past couple of years.*

Nurse: "Now this may hurt a little bit."

Me: "That's okay."

Nurse slowly slides the needle in.

As the needle slid in, I slowly raise my head and try to do my best to fight back the tears to stop them from rolling down the sides of my face. The needle went in so deep I swear it felt like it punctured my soul. It honestly felt like that needle was in my arm for an eternity, because I bit my bottom lip so hard I could taste blood in my mouth. I am still looking up at the ceiling as the nurse is saying, "We're almost done." I'm watching the needle fill up with my blood and I remember thinking, "You're taking my life."

My eyes are still tearing up, and my fists tighten up in anger as I try to figure out how I let my life get so bad, so fast. With my mind still racing, I start racking my brain, trying to understand where I went wrong in life to end up here. Then I finally realized that the major event that derailed my seemingly perfect life was when I met my ex-wife. The nurse tells me she is finished and slowly slides the needle out. She hands me a cotton swab and tells me to apply pressure on the hole until it stops bleeding. She also hands me the research drugs and tells me to swallow them. I do it and almost instantly feel different. The nurse tells me that she will be back to check my vitals in four hours.

After she walks away, all I keep asking myself is "How did I get here?" How did I go from making six figures while working at a law firm to being flat broke with tons of debt? How did I go from getting ready to build my first brand new home after graduating college to being homeless? How did I go from being a joyful, clean-cut businessman who drove his dream car to looking like a depressed bum who got his car repossessed, and now sleeps on cold floors and hard couches? How did I go from being the student body president of a major Christian university to not even knowing if I believe in God at all anymore? How did I get here?

Before you judge me, please give me the opportunity to explain my story in its entirety. Also, after you form your opinions, please keep them to yourself, because I have already made peace with myself over some of the wicked things I've done in my past. I've faced my fears and destroyed my demons, and I am not afraid to say that I was afraid more times than I would like to admit during this painful journey. I am writing this to let people know that they are not alone in what they feel. Whether you have also gone through a divorce, are recovering from a major heartbreak, or are currently in love, this book is for you. All the embarrassment this may bring me is worth it if this book even saves one marriage, or helps one unprepared couple realize that they should not get married.

## My Intentions

Sometimes people do things with the proper intentions, but they are interpreted in the wrong manner, so I want to make my intentions crystal clear from the start.

My intentions for this book are as follows:

1. To save marriages
2. To help couples who are courting or engaged figure out if they are ready for marriage
3. To help individuals detect red flags in their relationships before major marital mistakes are made

This book is *not* intended in any way, shape, or form to harm, defame, or shame my ex-wife, my ex-church, or my ex–in-laws. I wish them all the best in their endeavors.

# OUR FAMILY FOUNDATIONS

TO UNDERSTAND ANYTHING in its entirety, one must understand its origin; so to help everyone understand how our perception of marriage was built, I would like to briefly share a bit about our backgrounds.

On October 24, 1986, I was born as the last of four children to Edward and Fatmata Cavalli. My parents were from Sierra Leone, West Africa, where they grew up in a Muslim community and worked in diamond mines. Within this community, my grandfather on my dad's side was allowed eight wives. My father, being one of the only people able to read in his village, saved his money and set off for a better life in America after meeting my mother. He had to go to America alone because he did not have enough money at that time for them both. My father promised my mother that he would get established in America first, and then he would send for her to come when he properly prepared a place for them. He came to America with nothing, but he was taken in by an old Christian woman who helped him get on his feet, and taught him about the love of Jesus Christ. Through the love this old woman showed, my father converted to Christianity! Things in his life started aligning with ease, and then he was able to save enough money to send for my mother to come from Africa over two years after his arrival. Once my parents were reunited, they started having children on top of working several jobs and going to school full time.

By the time I was born, my parents were fairly settled into their careers. My father was a chemist, and my mother had just become a registered nurse. Along with their individual careers, my parents felt led in their hearts to start their first church the same year as my birth. My father said that God showed him dreams that I would pastor that church someday, and that he would do everything in his power to keep the church alive until I was ready to take it over.

In reference to marriage, being a part of my family as a child was a blessing and a curse all at the same time. It was a blessing because it was amazing to have a complete family. I loved having both my parents in my life, and both happily living under the same roof. In the second town that my father moved our family to, I was one of the only African American children that had their biological father at home. Now that I think about it, I was one of the only African American child who had a father figure at home at all for that matter. It was a blessing growing up in my home because there were no fights over money, adultery, or any fights at all for that matter between my parents. I can honestly say that I have *NEVER* seen or heard my parents ever fight or disrespect each other. It wasn't like they stepped out of the house and screamed at each other behind closed doors either. I watched them constantly resolve issues in front of me in a peaceful manner.

The reason they did not fight was not because we had an abundance of money or because our lives were picture-perfect. One of the many reasons they never fought was because their communication was phenomenal. The reason their communication was amazing was because they were both very mature individuals who knew how to disagree respectfully. My father and mother were both incredibly strong-willed people, but they had structure to their individual lives and to their marriage. As a child, I never had to question which parent was in charge. It was simple: they both were. They were matched intellectually, morally and spiritually. My father taught me that being matched in all major elements of life like this is what the Bible calls being "equally yoked". Dad taught me that if a man is unequally yoked to his wife, it is equivalent to an ox that is joined by the neck to another ox while plowing the fields. When two oxen are joined together at the neck, they need to be in simultaneous strides with one another. If those oxen are not in equal strides, the ox that tries to get ahead too quickly (the ambitious one) will break its neck. He said that in life, "Couples don't need to have the exact same dreams, but they do need to be going in the same direction in life." Two people will not end at the same destination if they cannot agree about what direction to go in.

Watching my parents interact as I grew up taught me that two people who loved each other could disagree without ever raising their voices or degrading the other partner. Observing their marriage through my eyes allowed my siblings and myself the privilege of witnessing, for lack of better terms, what a "perfect marriage" should be like.

That perception of a perfect marriage put me at a disadvantage for life as well because to a certain degree, I was ignorant to all the twisted lies and deception that I would later on be blindsided by when I got married. As a young child, many television shows did not make much sense to me because I could not comprehend why a man would leave his wife and kids. I couldn't understand why a man would ever cheat, beat, or mistreat his wife if every woman was as loyal and caring as my mother. I was naive to reality in some regards because "my reality" was so different from everyone else's.

During my childhood years, I realized that I would get invited over to my friends' houses for dinner more if I would stop asking dumb questions about where their dads were. I used to ask my friends why their parents were always yelling. My friends would just reply, "That's just how my parents talk to each other," and then we would go back outside to play. Once again, my reality was not in line with the rest of the neighborhood's reality. People talking calmly was what I was used to, while my friends were used to screaming all the time. As my friends and I grew up, I saw how aggressively they handled certain situations and how calmly I would naturally react to the same ones. I saw how my guy friends would mistreat their girlfriends, and I would see how my female friends would just take the abuse to keep their boyfriends around. There was no doubt in my mind that we were all mimicking our home situations, and were products of our environments.

Early on in my childhood, my parents told me how the world was full of sin and how the hearts of most of mankind were wicked. They told me that I could either be a young wise man or an old fool. My parents mentioned that I could either make the world better or worse by the decisions I chose to make for myself. During that same conversation, they advised me to never drink, smoke and to save my virginity until I was married. Then they both put their hands on my head and prayed with tears in their eyes that when their little boy became a man, he would not depart from their teachings. I listened to the plea they made with me, and I took heed to their instructions.

My ex-wife, whom I will refer to as Sara, came from a very different upbringing. From what I have gathered from the stories that Sara, her parents, and her siblings would tell me, Sara grew up in a quarrelsome home. Even though her parents were pastors as well, she witnessed many heated screaming matches between them. Arguments ranged from money issues to power struggles over authority between Sara's mother and father. The grandparents on her mother's side had a very verbally and physically abusive relationship. The grandfather on Sara's mother's side was also constantly in and out of jail for crimes that he would commit. Sara's uncles were also notorious for scamming people in the city of Chicago for millions of dollars. Her cousin was also charged with sleeping with an underage female, and also for scamming people for millions of dollars as well, but I didn't realize these family secrets until after Sara and I were married. I am stating these facts to make the point that we came from two very different worlds.

I want to note that it is completely fine if two people who love each other come from different backgrounds. That's one of the elements of life that make love beautiful! Those people would just need to know how to extract the good out of their bad situations and use it to become a new union. Much can be learned and gained from marrying someone who is opposite than yourself, but much can also be lost and destroyed in the process of becoming one. There is always a very delicate balance that needs to be sustained; otherwise, the outcome can be as dangerous as explosions from mixing the correct chemicals together at the wrong time. My dad always said that "The right thing at the wrong time will ruin you, and the wrong thing at the right time will also ruin you." Timing is everything.

# The Beginning of the End

O N OCTOBER 6, 2008, I met a girl named Sara Smith who one day was going to be my wife, and then my ex-wife. Before I even knew of her existence, I was friends with her brother, whom I will refer to as Chad from this point. Chad and I became friends at a private Christian university, where he just became a resident advisor (RA), and I was just leaving the (RA) position because I had just been elected student body president of the university. I was a senior, and Chad was a junior at this time. Chad told me that after I graduated, he would like to run for the presidency himself. We became quick friends, and I wanted to do my best to take him under my wing and leave the university in good hands after my departure. As Chad and I became better friends, I started letting him know more about my life goals and dreams. Soon afterward, Chad would try and tell me that his sister would be a perfect match for me, because her goals and my goals in life matched up so perfectly. I wasn't overly excited to meet her since I was getting a lot of pressure from all my different friends to meet their sisters. Chad was from Chicago, and during our college fall break session, he invited me out to his parents' home and church out there. Before the weekend that we were supposed to leave, Sara came up to our college to visit Chad and their other sister, whom I will refer to as Maria.

I remember the day I met Sara like it was yesterday. I was rushing across the campus in the rain after a heated meeting, heading to my office. Chad and Maria abruptly stopped me and introduced me to Sara. I wish I could say it was love at first sight, but it simply wasn't. At that moment, her hair didn't look washed, she had an old white tank top on and ripped jeans that were several sizes too big. Also, her nails and toes were not done, which is a major turnoff for me. I shook her hand quickly, told her it was nice to meet her. Then I headed right into my office.

The next time I saw her was a day later, and she looked a hundred times better. I guess Maria gave her a makeover, but she did manage to get my attention at that time. She looked beautiful now, but it was what she was saying that had my heart stop. Her dreams of going overseas and starting orphanages and constructing different methods of changing the world seemed incredible. They seemed even more amazing since it was exactly what I wanted to do and the way I wanted to do it. It was almost as if she was reading off a script, but now looking back, she probably was. Already blinded by love, I couldn't see what I was really being set up for. During the next couple days, Sara and I spent countless hours together, going to events, eating, and just laughing the entire time. Sara, her siblings, my best friend Mark, and I left for our fourteen-hour drive to Chicago to start our fall break session. We arrived the next day, to be greeted by Sara's parents. From this point, I will refer to Sara's father and mother as James (Jim) and Tiffany (Tiff). From the beginning, they seemed very nice and welcoming; but even at that time, something just didn't feel right about them.

After meeting her parents, things went from zero to one hundred really quickly. Sara and I were becoming fonder of each other, and her parents noticed that as well. During the time I was in Chicago for that fall break session, I also got the opportunity to visit their family's two churches that Sara's parents were pastors in. I also visited there 1-million-dollar city home and their 1.4-million-dollar lake home. The reason I knew how much they were was because Sara's family repeatedly talked about how much everything they had cost. Everything to them was status symbols. It was all about what people drove and what kind of watch or purse someone had. At first, I was a little curious as to how they acquired their wealth. I looked at myself as being an up-and-coming businessman, and I was always looking for new wisdom to be a better one. In passing, the father told me about how he did major deals in his real estate career throughout his life. I figured that the father was about fifty-five years old, so it all seemed to make logical sense. My father also had a secular career apart from the church that he pastored. However, my father had that career so that he never had to depend on getting money from the church. He was always able to sustain our family directly from his career in the science field. After finding out that information from Sara's father, I never bothered to ask anything else about how they made their money, because their family business was none of my business at this point in time.

Sara and I became closer and closer as my fall break session progressed. One night, as my break was coming to an end, Sara and I admitted that we had feelings toward each other and would like to be more than friends. As we confessed our feelings for each other, I thought that it would be wise to set some ground rules if we planned to be together in a long-distance relationship. I wanted to set ground rules because I have personally known some of the best and most respectful people to do the worst things in the wrong situations. I figured that if we can make a game plan together ahead of time, then we would not have to worry about offending each other or being in compromising situations. I really cared for Sara and believed that we could build a beautiful life together, so I wanted to give us every possible opportunity to succeed and flourish. One of the rules we agreed upon was that we would not hang out with either of our exes anymore. It just made sense in our logic. We figured that if we were already attracted to our exes once, it would be even easier to be tempted while being around them again. The other rule we agreed on was for neither of us to be alone with a friend from the opposite sex. Neither of us would feel comfortable with the other being alone with someone from the opposite sex alone, because it could easily give off the wrong impression to that friend. We both knew that even when lines are clearly drawn in the sand sometimes people still try things when they are alone. We were free to hang out with groups of people, but just not individuals alone. We both felt great about the rules we came up with together. We now had a mutual understanding and were excited to see what the future had in store for us!

My father always taught me about the Bible principle that a person will reap what he sows. The modern-day translation of this ancient Proverb would be, "What goes around comes around." I bring this up because I always hoped that if I ever had a daughter, the young man who wanted to court her would be respectful and go about it in an honorable manner. Due to the fact that I expected those actions to be done to me in the future, I wanted to set those positive actions in motion at the present time. The next morning when I woke up, I asked Sara's parents if I could speak to them privately about something. I sat them down and explained to them how Sara and I have developed feelings for one another, and that with their blessings, we would like to pursue a relationship. For two hours, we spoke about why I would be a good fit for her and why she would be a good fit for me. I also gave them full reign to ask me absolutely anything about my life and my family. They appreciated me giving them that liberty, where they proceeded to ask me a flood of questions ranging from if I had ever done drugs to how many people I had sex with up to that time. They were relieved and ecstatic to know that I had never done any drugs in my life and was a virgin up to that point as well. They then told me how happy they were to have a quality man dating their daughter, and not one of the drug-addicted boys she usually hangs around with. Her parents continued in telling me how many men were always after her from the time she was young. That did not alarm me at that time because I figured that there is nothing wrong with people admiring a person. However, there is something wrong with giving your body to all your admirers. I just assumed she was a wholesome, level-headed young lady. I never thought to ask her those questions. Not asking her those important questions was a mistake, but I didn't know it at the time. Sara joined us shortly after our conversation, and she was happy to know that everyone was in agreement and joyful that we would be together. At this point, all Sara's siblings had also given me their blessings to pursue their sister Sara as well.

During this fall break, I was also introduced to countless members of Sara's church, but there was one gentleman who Sara's mother insisted that I meet. For the sake of privacy, I will refer to this man as Dan. Dan was a very well-dressed and well-spoken African American man. He apparently worked for a major law firm in Chicago and held a prestigious position with them. I spoke to Dan for quite a bit of time, and then Sara's mom said to Dan, "Well, do you like him?" Dan said, "Of course I like him. This kid is really sharp." Dan asked when I was graduating from college, and I told him that I would be graduating in May of that year. He gave he his card and told me to call him a month before I graduated if I wanted a great job playing with the big boys in business. I immediately put that card in my wallet and left with Sara.

It came to the last night of my fall break before I had to drive back to my college. I told Sara about a major event I was throwing with my VP the following month, and how I would like her and her parents to come. I also told Sara that I would visit her every month until I graduated. Keep in mind that it was a fourteen-hour drive each way from Tulsa to Chicago, but my word was my word. Chad, Maria, and my best friend Mark packed the car up and we left for Tulsa.

Before I got back to campus, I changed my status on Facebook from "Single" to "In a Relationship." I just wanted to make it clear that I was taken because I knew how often certain females would make passes at me. I didn't want there to be any confusion about who I was devoted to. My father and mother taught me to make it clear to people where your heart lies, so I did just that. By the time I got back to campus, I was instantly being attacked by females saying all kinds of mean things about my relationship. Most of the females who were attacking me were just saying that I never paid them any attention. I had girls in my campus office crying about how they feel like I led them on, and then I had to have them escorted out by my secretaries. Thank you, Jess Lo and Sara Eh (My secretaries). To say the least, things got a little crazy, but I had already made up my mind about who I wanted.

The next month rolled around, and Sara and her family drove down from Chicago to come to our campus event. The event went well, and after it was done, I jumped off the stage and gave Sara some flowers I purchased. Sara's whole family and I went out to eat afterward. At the end of the meal, Sara and I wanted to spend some alone time since we haven't seen each other for a month, and up to that point, we had not kissed yet. I didn't want to kiss her during my Fall Break because I wanted to let her know that this wasn't just about physical attraction. Maria brought her car to the restaurant, but she let Sara and I use it since I did not have a car at this time. Sara and I got in Maria's car, and I drove to the corner of the parking lot, right before joining the stream of traffic. I leaned over to say something to her while my foot was on the breaks, and I ended up accidently kissing her. I somehow slipped my foot off the breaks and hit the gas and headed right into oncoming traffic. We literally almost died, but then my *Fast and Furious* instincts kicked in (thanks Vin Diesel), and I somehow pull off a U-turn while weaving through several cars. I get us to safety, and we drive to a nearby lake and just laugh at what just happened for about ten minutes. She said, "I know I was a good kisser, but I didn't know I was that good." She had a cocky side to her that I liked, among many other things that I adored about her.

For the next several hours, we just enjoyed laughing, kissing, holding hands, and talking about our future. When I saw that it was getting late, I dropped Sara off at the hotel that her parents were staying at, but I had to sleep in the car. Since I went to a strict Christian university there were rules that only allowed students to come back on campus before certain hours of the night, so since I missed the cut-off time, I was going to have to sleep in the car, in the parking lot of Sara's hotel. Right as I was about to fall asleep, I heard a knock on my driver's window, and I jumped up. It was Sara telling me that her dad wasn't going to let me sleep in the car, but I told her, "It's okay, I watched a lot of Bruce Lee growing up, and I can fight!" She convinced me to come up to the room. For some reason, when we got up to the room, Tiff and Jim were sleeping in different beds. Sara went to lay down in the bed with her mom, and the dad made me lie on the floor right next to his bed. Yes, you guessed it—that was the most awkward night of my *entire* life. I just stared at the ceiling all night because her dad was snoring like a human chainsaw. There were several times throughout the night that I contemplated smothering Jim with a pillow, but I showed him mercy since I really loved Sara. In the morning, we all ate breakfast, and I saw her family off on their road trip back to Chicago.

At this point, Sara was perfect in my eyes and could do no wrong. She was loyal, intelligent, caring, and focused. I couldn't be any happier with the way our relationship was going. We talked every day and prayed together every night. I just wanted to be a good leader for us and make sure that we stayed focused on what needed to be done so that we could have a successful future together.

Over the next couple of months, things carried on flawlessly, and progression was in full effect. Sara and I still spoke about twice a day. We still prayed every night. We even took turns visiting each other back and forth every month until it was getting close to graduation. As time progressed, we fell deeper and deeper in love. I just felt like, "This is the woman that I want to spend the rest of my life with," and she felt the same way toward me. Even though we both loved each other equally and wanted to spend the rest of our lives together, we had different time lines of when we wanted to get married. We were both going to graduate around the same time, but I wanted to originally stay in school until I had my doctorate. I explained to Sara the importance of timing and how even the right thing at the wrong time could be a combination for chaos.

She told me that she understood where I was coming from, and that I made a very valid point. Sara originally wanted to get married right after our graduations. Coincidentally, the next day, I get a call from her dad "just wanting to talk" to me about my future plans and how Sara fit into them. I told Jim that I planned on getting my doctorate, and that marriage was not in my immediate future. In a very friendly way, Jim asked why I couldn't get my doctorate while I was married. He explained to me how he was able to get his doctorate while he was married with kids and building a church at the same time. I thought to myself how that was a great point. Then I also told him how having a safety net of money was incredibly important to me. I told Jim, "After watching the movie *Pursuit of Happiness*, I promised myself that I would never, ever let my children or wife worry where money was coming from. In my mind, I had set a goal to have at least twelve thousand dollars in my savings untouched at all times by the time I got married. Jim told me that my thought process was commendable, but it's not necessary to have that much money in the bank when you are first getting married. He explained how Tiff and he survived very humbly in the beginning stages of marriage, and that taught them how to manage money better in the end. I couldn't argue with the fact that Jim had decades more of life experience than me. I also had no reason to believe that he would ever want to deceive me into doing something that would so directly impact his daughter if things went wrong. I thought about everything Jim said to me for the next full week. I couldn't really find any flaws in his arguments. To top it off, this was the man that I trusted like a dad and spiritual mentor. He was also telling me that it was okay to marry his daughter earlier than I ever could have expected. Several days later, I called Sara and told her that I'm open to exploring the idea of getting married before I get my doctorate. She screamed on the phone for what seemed like forever! She kept saying, "Really? Really? I can't believe this! Really? You're the best!" She was very excited, and I was too!

But a couple of months before my graduation, there were a couple of hiccups that we encountered. The first obstacle we had to overcome was her meeting my family. It was very difficult to arrange the meeting between Sara and my family since Sara, my family, and I were all in three different states. During one of the times when I revisited Sara, Jim overheard me talking about how I was going to be visiting my family the following month. Jim came to me and said that would be a great time for Sara to meet my family. I wasn't inviting Sara at this time because I haven't seen my own family for quite some time. I wanted to be able to spend some family time with my family alone and not drop any bombs on them since they haven't seen me in so long. Sara's dad was very persistent with making sure that Sara came with me, so I finally just gave in. Then later on that day, the dad said he would also like to meet my parents and went on to tell me that he had already booked the flight for him and Tiff. I felt like that was really pushy, but I figured this man loves me and wants to get to know my family too. What could possibly go wrong? The answer: *everything*, everything could go wrong.

From the time Sara's family landed in New Jersey to meet my family, there was tension because her dad thought it would be funny to make an African joke to break the ice with my father. Not funny. Mix a lame, slightly offensive joke about someone's homeland with already unwanted guests, and you have yourself a very awkward forty-five-minute ride from the airport. When we got home, her mom said that we live in a much better neighborhood than she expected, which already took my parents from zero to sixty in three seconds. I mean, my parents are not rich by any means, but at this stage in life, they are far from poor. My parents actually bought a brand-new home and were the first owners of this house that was located in a predominately caucasian neighborhood. That was bad joke number two. As you could imagine, these bad jokes just kept on flying without her parents taking a hint that they were not funny at all. So a day goes by, and my parents start to find some common ground with Sara's parents. The jokes actually began to become funnier, and there was peace in my parent's home.

We get to the last night before Sara and her family were about to leave, and Jim came to me and said, "We should all talk about how you and Sara will get married." I advised Jim not to bring it up yet since I have not gotten the opportunity to properly prepare my parents for this. Jim agreed, so I thought that I had nothing to worry about at dinner. Dinnertime rolls around, and my mom cooked a big feast for the last night. Conversations were going well at the table, food was being passed, and then Jim spoke. Jim took it upon himself to say, "Leo, I know you told me not to tell, but I'm just too excited to hold it in any longer."

As soon as those words were uttered from Jim's mouth, a chain of uncommon events happened to my body. First, I threw up in my mouth a little bit, which was followed by my heart stopping, and I finished off with urinating on myself. Okay, none of those three things really happened, but I wouldn't be surprised if they did because I was that scared. My dad, in his deep African, coming-to-America accent, said, "What is it that you can't wait to tell me, Jim?" Jim continued on by saying, "Leo and Sara are in love . . . and are going to get married . . . soon!" At this point, I started to hallucinate from all the fear, which caused a chemical imbalance in my brain. I started hallucinating so bad that I'm pretty sure I saw the Grim Reaper sitting across from me at the dinner table. I was sure of it because Mr. Reaper asked me to pass the candied yams, along with my soul, because I knew I was about to die. I also tried to figure out if there was enough mashed potatoes on my plate to drown myself in and just end the misery that was about to befall us all.

My dad must have already considered me dead, and forgot that I ever existed, because he asked Jim, "Which Leo was getting married?" Jim pointed across the table and said, "That Leo!" I looked behind me, and to my surprise, there was no other Leo that he could be referring to. My dad began to do his chuckle, which was the same chuckle he would do after he read my report card in elementary school and decided to whip me. I knew it was about to get ugly, but for Jim's sake, I'm glad my dad no longer kept his spear in the house. Otherwise, Jim would be hanging over our fireplace right next to the lion head my dad claimed that he killed in Africa. Yes, my dad told me that he killed a lion with his bare hands, while on his way to school, after walking twenty miles in the snow, barefoot. On a side note, that story never made sense to me, but I never had the courage to question him.

My father then stopped laughing, and everyone at the table got graveyard quiet as my father began to go into his "Pastor Martin Luther King" mode. My dad looked Jim in the eyes and said," My son Leonardo, my last born, will *not* be marrying your daughter. My son is meant to be a doctor and change the world, and this will only slow down his dreams. My son Leonardo is a king, and your daughter is a distraction sent to detour him off track. You may be able to trick him for a moment, but I see right through you. God has not shown your daughter to be the wife for my son. When Leonardo realizes whatever little spell you put on him, he will return back home." My dad said he was done talking about this and then asked me to pass the candied yams that I had previously passed to the Grim Reaper. Jim laughed and said, "Well, that didn't go as planned." I tried to chime in and help my dad understand all the options, and he cut me off and yelled, "I'm done with this rubbish talk!" When my dad is done with something, he is really done with it.

It was a very quiet dinner from that moment on. Sara's family left the next day, and my parents said that they really wanted to have a serious talk with me. They told me that they look forward to me getting married someday, but they felt that something was genuinely not right about Sara's family. My parents were confused as to why any sensible family would be in such a rush to give their daughter into marriage. My dad threw out the idea that maybe she was sick with some kind of illness. He also mentioned that Sara might be very promiscuous and the parents may not want her to have a child by bad person. My mother told me that Sara was a witch. I jokingly told my parents how I know it's hard to lose your favorite child, but I would visit them when I could. It seemed that Sara's family's bad jokes had rubbed off on me, because my parents were not laughing at all. My dad mentioned that I should do some research on their family because they came off too odd and too pushy. He finally said that God told him that I wasn't ready at this time. Looking back now, I figure this was God trying to keep me from making a major mistake. Hearing my dad say that just infuriated me, and I immediately went into defense mode. I made up my mind that I was going to show my parents and God that I was ready—show them that I was my own man. I thought that my parents were honestly over exaggerating, but nonetheless, I told them that I would keep a look out for any "suspicious" activities. I returned to my school to finish my senior year.

Things just weren't the same after that visit home with my parents because now we all knew that there was a major obstacle to overcome with winning my parents over. Even though Sara said she was fine, I could hear how disappointed she was in her voice. No woman likes to hear that they aren't good enough for the man they love. Even her parents were hurt by my dad's words and, from time to time, would try to call and reason with him. There were times where my dad would call me and tell me about how he made Sara's mom cry on the phone. My dad is a very loving man, but he will be ruthless if you threaten his children's future. For months, my dad and I had full-out yelling matches on the phone where he threatened to disown me, and I told him I never wanted to speak to him again. It even got to the point where my dad told me that my mother and him were not coming to the wedding and will disown any of my siblings if they go either. I called his bluff and told him that he wouldn't dare do that. My dad kept saying that I was too young, and I asked him to give me the perfect marriage age. I knew there wasn't one because every single person on the earth is different and has different maturity levels at various ages. There is no cookie-cutter answer. I even stated a verse that he taught me from Ephesians 5:31 in the Bible that says, "For this reason a man will leave his father and mother to be united with his wife, and the two will become one flesh." I kept telling my dad that he needed to stop being so controlling and be more supportive.

One thing you should know about me is that when I set my mind on something, it's going to get done! I get into this zone, get tunnel vision, and I get extremely focused. I continue to charge at my target until I see a breakthrough. I feel like if I played bloody knuckles with a brick wall, the wall would lose. I've always prided myself on the fact that I have never given up on anything in my life that I have chosen to commit to. Now that I have chosen to commit to Sara, there was no turning back now. I had officially made up my mind that Sara was who I wanted to spend the rest of my life with, even if it would cost the relationship with my father and family. I couldn't see why my family just couldn't be happy for me. By their standards, I had done everything by the book, and my parents should be proud of me. Even up to that point, I never touched alcohol, never smoked, never indulged in drugs, was doing very well academically, and was still saving my virginity until marriage. I just figured that there was no pleasing my father, so I just went numb and focused on what made me happy. I remember telling my dad that if he didn't come to my wedding, he could lose my number, and that he would never see my children. I was now motivated to marry Sara for two reasons. The first reason was because I genuinely loved Sara with all my heart and believed she was the one for me. She was incredibly supportive during that stressful senior year of college. That senior year, I was taking over twenty credit hours, along with constantly being pulled out of class to help pick an actual president for our university. The university was in a major transitional stage. On top of that, I was trying to figure out the rest of my life while going to war with my family over the woman I loved. Sara was great at calming me down and simplifying things so

I didn't get overwhelmed. The second reason I wanted to marry Sara was to show my father that I did not need him, and that I knew how to make great decisions by myself. I now know that my second reason for marrying Sara should have never been used for any sort of motivation.

Graduation day was now less than a month away. I was excited, but also very nervous about the future. Luckily enough, I already had a job locked down with Dan from the law firm, whom I met in Chicago during my first visit. My biggest concern at that time was how I would keep my family and Sara's family from killing each other at this second encounter during my graduation. My biological family was obviously flying out to see their son, but at this point, Sara's parents also considered me a son as well, and they all wanted to support their boy on the his big day. Graduation day was also so important because a month before that time, during my most recent visit to Chicago, Jim had convinced me that the best time to propose would be right after my graduation. He said it would be perfect because both families would be there, and it would already be a joyous occasion. Once again, please keep in mind that I talked to Jim three times a week, and I now considered him a business mentor, spiritual advisor/ pastor, dad, and best friend. Never in my mind did I question Jim's motives for wanting to move things so quickly. I thought that he was just really excited to have me as part of his family and didn't want to lose me as a son. That was just one of many times that I was overly optimistic, and it turned around to bite me.

Fast forward to the day before my college graduation. The ring I bought just arrived in the mail because I had it overnighted from her parents' jeweler. If you're wondering how I knew what ring Sara wanted, I'll tell you. During the second to last visit I made to Chicago to see Sara, her mom had a diamond fall out of one of her thirty-thousand-dollar bracelets. Once again, the only reason I knew the cost was because of how much they talked about it. So Jim and Tiff said they were going to their family jeweler to get it fixed. The parents invited Sara and me to come with them, so we went. When we arrived, I was immediately intimidated because everything in the store looked "arm and leg" expensive. I didn't want to touch anything. I didn't even want to sit down, for fear I might break something. As the bracelet was being fixed, Jim said, "How about you ladies try on some of the jewelry?" Sara looked at me as if to ask for permission, and I just faked a smile as if to say yes. In my head, I was really saying, "Girrrrl, if you don't put those damn diamonds *down!*"

Sara started trying on necklaces. Then she started trying on bracelets, and then somehow made her way over to the wedding rings. I took a deep breath as she called the jeweler over to open the case. The jeweler walked over, and my heart was beating out of my chest. My hands became grossly sweaty, and I began to get light-headed as he approached the glass. He said, "Now which one would you like to see, Sara?" Sara paused for a moment while her eyes scanned over the vast selection of rings. Sara used her finger and started going left to right to help her narrow in on the one she wanted. I was standing on her side, trying to move her hand with my mind like one of those medal claws that grab the stuffed animals at the arcade. Then as Sara tapped on the glass, all I heard her say was, "Ooooh, I love this one! Can you pull it out for me to see it?" This was where I would usually make a "that's what she said" joke about it, but my mind was so discombobulated that I didn't have time to. The jeweler pulled out this huge gorgeous ring, and all I started to see was red. I wasn't sure if I was seeing red because I was so nervous that I popped a blood vessel in my eye, or because I was looking into the future and seeing my bank statements for the next two years after trying to pay this ring off. Sara slipped on the ring, looked at her parents and then me, and said, "I'm soooooo in love with it! It already feels like it's mine!" The jeweler started raving about how amazing it looked on her, and I was trying to figure out a way to burn the store down and not go to jail.

I asked Sara to let me see her hand so I could "see how it fits." I was secretly trying to see the price, which everyone was obviously ignoring. I managed to smoothly flip the tag to see the cost, but oddly enough, someone mistakenly left their phone number on the price tag. Then I realized that wasn't a phone number, but the actual price. The price—and everything in the room started spinning. I asked the jeweler if this price was correct, and he confirmed that my nightmare was, in fact, now a reality. Since I knew that there was no getting out of this, I immediately went into sales mode and tried to get him to lower the price. He said that since Sara was like family, he would give me the family discount. Even with the discount, the cost of the ring and the diamond band came out to a little over ten thousand dollars. Even though I wasn't excited about the price, I was excited to marry this woman that I loved. When I also looked at the big picture, this was going to be my wife someday, so it's not like she was just some random girl that I'll never see again. In my mind, I always said to myself that if my wife leans on me, I will lean on God, and everything will work out. Since the ring cost so much, I figured I would have to lean on God harder than Morgan Freeman in the movie *Eastside High*. I have always watched my father rise to the occasion if my mother ever wanted something, so I was determined to do the same, no matter what the cost.

Travel back with me to the night before graduation. As I mentioned, the ring had just arrived, so I was happy about that. My family and Sara's family had flown in for my hooding ceremony. After the hooding ceremony, my parents went back to their hotel room, where I joined them for a moment. I sat them down and told them about my plans to get engaged the day after graduation. My dad told me how disappointed he was, and my mom just started crying and started talking to my dad in their native language. I'm not exactly sure what she was saying, but it doesn't take a rocket scientist to know that she was also deeply disappointed in my decision to go through with it. I told my parents that I was not there to consult with them, but just to inform them about what I was going to do. I left their room and went back to my dorm to get rest before graduation day.

It was now graduation day, and I was excited and nervous just like everyone else that day. I was backstage, getting ready like the rest of the student body, and then came out to find my seat. All the normal actions of a graduation took place. We stood for the national anthem. Speeches were given, names were called, while other names were called incorrectly and beach balls were being thrown. In the midst of it all, I looked up in the stands and saw my families blowing kisses to me and rooting for me as I tried to stay focused on enjoying that day. I wanted to really enjoy my graduation day and not let tomorrow's engagement event eclipse the glory of my shining moment which was at hand.

The usher then signaled for my row to rise, and we funneled out in a single file line. The lady in front of me went up to get her diploma, and it was about to be my time. I was praying that I won't trip and that I would take a good picture in the big rush. I was also praying that the announcer would pronounce my last name correctly because I was pretty sure my dad could still throw a spear from where he was standing in the crowd, and wouldn't think twice about doing it. My name was called, the announcer nailed my actual African name, and the crowd went wild! I walked on stage, dominated the picture, grabbed my diploma, pointed to my dad and mom, and mouthed, "We did it!" Then I pointed to Sara and mouthed, "This is for us," as Sara mouthed back, "I love you." As I looked at her mouthing those words, I just thought to myself, "*tomorrow, I am either going to make the best or the worst decision of my life.*"

Right before I left the stage, I just looked around for a second because I wanted to really embrace that moment. I walked down from the stage and rejoined my classmates. I gave a big sigh and said, "One major event down, and one more to go for this weekend." All the names finally got called, and tassels were switched from one side of the cap to the other. Hats were thrown, and I left to go to my little after-party. Both of our families were there and seemed to be getting along. The celebration went well into the night, and then everyone went back to their hotels.

The next morning when I woke up, I just felt uneasy, so I stayed in bed for a bit more. I later shook it off and got hyper about the day. I saw my parents one last time while they were in Tulsa and took them to the airport to see them off. They begged me not to get engaged to Sara, but I just remained quiet as I drove and dropped them off. Now it was time to focus on distracting Sara and getting ready for this proposal. I had worked incredibly hard for the last month to incorporate every single thing Sara told me she liked into this proposal. I made all my calls, made sure everyone was in position and knew their lines. Then I set the plan in motion. Everything went as planned, and then it was time to propose. I reached in my back pocket and got ready to get on one knee, but I forget which knee I was supposed to get on for a second. We laughed, and then I got on my left knee.

I recited a poem I wrote her, and then I spoke from my heart for a bit, and then I asked her to marry me. While crying, she screamed, "YES!!!" There aren't many situations that would scare a man more than getting on one knee, (the left knee) and asking the woman he loves to marry him. There are also not many feelings that compare with the joy a man feels when the woman he love tells him that she accepts his offer. We later joined her family for a big dinner celebration I put together. After dinner, we drove back to the lake that we had our first kisses at. We just held hands and kept looking at each other, saying,

"We're engaged, we're really engaged. You're my fiancée!" That night I also gave Sara an extra key to the car I just bought as a graduation present to myself. It was a black on black Cadillac CTS with beautiful shiny rims. I had been saving up forever for it, and I was finally able to buy it a week before my graduation. I just wanted Sara to know that now everything that was mine was hers. I loved Sara like love was the only feeling that I ever knew, and I couldn't wait to spend the rest of my life with my new fiancée.

The next morning, Sara's entire family and I woke up, packed up all of our cars, and did our last road trip to Chicago to start our new life together. For fourteen hours, Sara and I just held hands, laughed and talked about how great life was going to be. We talked about everything on that ride, from wedding colors to baby names. When we finally arrived at their home, Maria, Sara's sister, said, "Welcome home, Leo." It just meant a lot to me to hear that. We all lived in Sara's parents' house for that summer. My new life had begun. Within twenty-four hours, I went through two of the biggest changes in life thus far. I was now an engaged graduate/alumni!

We all unpacked our cars, and I got settled in. That weekend, we just relaxed and enjoyed family time on the lake since it was a beautiful summer. I started my new position at the law firm that following Monday. I met the entire team of paralegals and all the lawyers. Everyone was very welcoming even though I was the youngest person in the firm. I was now in the real world, with a real job. I really had a woman to take care of and a family to plan for, so I had the focus and determination of a laser beam. I spent long nights learning everything I could about our company and our clients, because I wanted to be the very best agent in the company. I promised Sara that I would provide and protect our family, and that's exactly what I was going to do! I hit the ground running with the firm, and my first month's earnings were more than enough to completely pay off the ring, so I did! I only got better with the job as time progressed, which resulted in more money. My dad and I would still talk from time to time. He was disappointed in my decision, but was proud that I was making money and taking care of business like a grown man. Months had passed, money had grown, and wedding decisions were being made. I was also saving a lot of money because Sara and I were still living with her parents in their huge home. I was aggressively looking for apartments with Sara, while her parents kept on insisting that we live with them even after we got married. I politely and repeatedly declined their offer. I appreciated them letting me stay with them for that summer, but I always enjoyed taking care of myself. I've worked from the age of thirteen so that I didn't have to ask my parents for anything. If I wanted something, I'm going to find a way to work hard and get it, period. Jim would make the offer for me to stay with them at least twice a week until I sternly had to tell him that I do not want to live in another man's home after getting married. Jim finally said that he respects my decision and backed down.

But before Sara and I ever even started looking for apartments, Jim put the thought in our head that it would be great if we built our first home. Jim said, "Leonardo, you're making more than enough money, and now would be the perfect time for it." Once again, I trusted Jim because he was a business mentor to me, as well as my soon-to-be father-in-law. We found a builder. We found a spot to put the house on, and I even paid $1,500 for the blueprints. My dad randomly called me and said that God had put me on his heart. He asked me what was new, and I told him of my plans to build a house. My dad ripped me a new one and said that Jim was leading me on the fast path to destruction. My dad brought up several great points that made complete sense of why it was not wise to build at this time. The market was still down, and you could get houses for almost 50 percent off what they were originally going for. I told Jim that I was no longer building the house, and we got in a huge argument. Sara was disappointed, but she understood my side since I would be paying for everything. It meant a lot to me to see Sara take my side over her father's because I was doing this for us and wanted to protect us financially. The next day at breakfast, Jim apologized to me and said he was just really excited to say that his daughter and son were building a home. I should have noticed right there how much Jim liked to brag on the things he had and what his family was doing. I guess I was just blinded by the love and the lights.

Beside that little episode, everything was perfect with Sara and I. We were loving life and getting closer every day. However, on one particular day, everything I thought about Sara changed. We woke up on Saturday morning like any other weekend, but on that day, the rest of Sara's family were at the lake house, while we were at the everyday home. Sara and I ate breakfast and then went in the lower level of their home to watch TV. We were quietly watching TV when I literally just felt something wrong in my gut, like right in my soul. At random times in my life, I would have mini-visions. I don't know how they happen or what triggers them, but they just help me see what's not being said. I can't control when they happen, but they just happen. When Sara and I were watching TV that day, I had one of those visions. I just remember everything else in the room turning black around me and then saw I a mini-vision of Sara in the car with a guy. I saw the guy's clothes, car, tattoos and then I saw them kissing. I also heard the name *Devon*. When this five-second vision was done, I looked at Sara and said, "Sara, who is Devon?" Sara looked at me in shock as if she was looking at a ghost and then started crying harder than I've ever seen anyone cry in my life. I jump up off the couch and say,

"Who the hell is Devon?"

SARA: (Hysterically crying, explains while I'm pacing back and forth in anger) "He was just a friend."

ME: "Well, did you guys ever hook up while we were together?"

SARA: (Puts her hands over her face and nods her head yes as she continues to cry).

At this point, I was on fire because she lied to me. In a matter of seconds, I put it together that this all happened during the one night that Sara's phone "wasn't working" when we were still having a long distance relationship. Even though Sara said that they just hung out, I knew it had to be more because any other time she was hanging out with guys, she would tell me, just like I would tell her if I was hanging out with a group of girls. She purposely kept this hang-out session a secret because there was clearly more that went on.

ME: "Sara, you broke our rules. You broke our trust you. You're a fucking liar, and I literally can't stand to look at you right now. How can you lie to someone like that? Damn, don't you even have a heart? I fought my whole family for you. I'm halfway across the country in this strange-ass city for you. I took this job for you. I bought that stupid, expensive-ass ring for you. I really cared for you . . . I really cared. For what? For you to fuck me over like this? You let me get on one knee and propose to you when you knew that you were keeping secrets. Why the fuck would you do that? The worst part about it is, you never would have openly confessed it to me, and you would have just kept living a lie. This shit is so embarrassing. Oh my god. Where do we even go from here? I don't even know you right now. What do I even tell my family?

You know what? I'm not going to tell my family; I'm telling yours. Yep, I'm going tell your parents what a crazy liar they raised!"

Keep in mind that the entire time I was yelling, she was grabbing my shirt and hands saying, "I'm so sorry. I'm sorry. It wasn't supposed to be like this. I'm so sorry. I'll never do it again. I made a mistake. Please don't leave. I promise to God I'm a good woman." My anger at that time made me deaf to any other impulsive lies she spewed out. I ran upstairs, grabbed my keys, and walked out of the house, slamming the door. Sara came running out after me, screaming, "Where are you going?" I just said, "To tell your parents that you're a liar and that we are *not* getting married."

I jumped in my car, and she quickly jumped into my passenger seat. I told her to get out because I was done with her. She tried to get the keys out of my hand and stop me from putting the key in the ignition. I was strong enough to hold her off with one hand and then use my other hand to start the car. Her neighbor was outside witnessing all this. I started the car and slammed on the gas to take off. Sara was trying to slap me in the face and was grabbing the steering wheel. While driving and trying to hold her back with my right arm, I said, "Are you crazy? Are you trying to kill us? Sit down!" I made a dumb decision to aggressively speed up to whip Sara back in her seat, and it did scare her enough to make her put on her seat belt. I finally made it onto one of the main roads, and she finally calmed down with the slaps and just slouched in her seat, crying with her hands over her face. She said, "My life is over. You're going to hurt my parents so bad if you tell them. They are not going to let me be the children's pastor anymore. This will be so embarrassing if my churches find out. I wish I could just disappear. I'm sorry, but please don't tell." I realized that out of all the people she was scared to hurt, I wasn't mentioned as one of them. I said, "You're just talking foolishness. You'll literally say anything right now so that I don't tell your parents who you really are. Do you think that by saying sorry that all the past can be corrected?" I continued to drive.

As I was speeding toward her lake home I was having the most extreme internal battle. I thought about all the good times we had, but I also thought about how she lied. I thought of all the laughs and love we shared, and all the great memories we've already made. I thought about how we were supposed to have a family. Thoughts of how much I still loved her kept replaying in my head. I just wanted peace. I loved Sara, and she was the last person in the world I wanted to fight with. There were also various occasions where she has had my back and been great to me. I was overwhelmed with different emotions, and I just didn't know the right thing to do, so I pulled over into a random open parking lot and parked. She undid her seat belt, grabbed the keys out the ignition, and straddled me in the driver's seat. At this point, I wasn't even trying to fight with her anymore. It just all seemed like a bad nightmare. I just wanted her to lie to me and tell me she wasn't going to do it anymore. Sara started kissing all over me, telling me how sorry she was and how it would never happen again. Deep down inside, I think I already knew that wasn't actually going to be the last time, but in that moment of confusion, the lies felt like warm bandages over fresh wounds. I honestly invested so much emotionally and financially that I just didn't want to have to restart with someone new. I know now that, that shouldn't have been a reason to stay.

Out of the corner of my eye, I see Sara's parents come speeding into the parking lot we were parked at. Her parents parked their car, and they jumped out. Sara ran into her mom's arms, and Jim came to speak to me. He asked me what was wrong, and I told him how his daughter lied to me and how I felt betrayed. Jim looked at Sara and said, "Sara, is this true? Did you break an agreement that you both made?" Sara nodded, cried, and then buried her head in her mother's chest. Sara's mother said, "Well, what was the agreement?" I told her parents that the agreement was that we wouldn't hang out alone with any exes or opposite gender friends alone. Sara's mother tried to defend Sara and talked about how Sara technically didn't do anything wrong, but before she could finish, Jim yelled at Tiff. Jim said, "No! Fair is fair, and Sara lied and broke Leo's trust. Sara is completely wrong here." Jim saying that meant the world to me because he kept a promise to me that he made when I first started dating Sara. Sara's parents promised that if she and I ever got into an argument, they would not choose sides or treat her special. At the time, it seemed too good to be true, but seeing Jim correct his wife and daughter in front of me gave me no doubt that I would be okay. Jim pointed at Sara and said, "I'm disappointed that you would do this. We raised you better than that. If Leo chooses to leave you, I would not blame him." Then Jim looked at me and said, "Leonardo, what are you deciding to do? Is the engagement off?" I looked up for a moment, took a deep breath, and then said, "No, no it's not." Sara ran into my arms, and I embraced her. Jim walked over and put his arm around both of us and said, "I'm sorry." We all traveled back home, and I just numbed myself and acted like nothing ever happened.

You may be wondering why I was so mad after one lie. The answer is that I absolutely hate liars. Once a person lies, it makes everything that person said or did for anyone questionable. It makes me uneasy because I never know what someone's motives are after that. I've cut close friends off because I've caught them in lies. I feel like I'm such an approachable person that if someone admits to something upfront, then I know that person is truly sorry. If I catch someone lying, and they had time and chances to come clean, then I feel like they are okay with living a lie. Those are the people that I want nothing to do with. You never know when they are actually telling the truth or not, and I would rather live alone than be surrounded by liars.

Looking back at that situation now, I should have taken that chance to run for the hills. Some of my other mentors have taught me not to believe what people say they are but believe who people show you they are. Life has now taught me that some people are just pieces of crap, and I do believe that people have the ability to change, but they also possess the ability to stay the same. Each individual has to realize that they are taking a gamble when they are waiting for their partner to change. If you are married, do your best to stick it through, but if you are not married yet, then you still have the open option to leave after a certain point in time. I had a friend who waited eleven years for her boyfriend to change, and he never did. She will never get those eleven years of her life back, and her partner left her for another woman. When someone does something wrong the first time, it can be considered a mistake. When someone does the same thing wrong the second time, it is now a decision. Unfortunately, Sara was a bad decision maker, but I just didn't know it at that time since this was the first offense I caught her in.

A couple weeks after that lying incident happened, Sara and I went back to being regular old us. We were back to laughing and loving each other all day and every day. Life was good again. I just got approved for my first apartment that Sara and I loved. I was excelling at work, and a wedding day was even set for October 16. We were doing insane amounts of wedding planning, and surprisingly, it was a lot of fun picking out things with my fiancée. The food-tasting part was the most fun for me! We were just having a lot of fun doing everything together.

Sara and I were also doing marriage counseling with her parents since they were our pastors. I know now that, that was a major mistake, but I just didn't know it back then. I don't ever advise parents to be the only marriage counseling a couple goes to. That just isn't the wisest move. Jim and Tiff were actually the ones fighting the most through the whole wedding preparation stage. There were times when I saw them mad at each other for days because they couldn't agree on what church members to invite to the wedding. Sara and I sent out the wedding invitations and even sent one to my parents in hopes it would help them realize how real this was. There were so many changes happening so quickly in our lives, but we were able to balance everything gracefully while we transitioned from one season of life into the next. Everything was good in our world, that is, until our next big fight.

As I had mentioned, business was going extremely well. I had an idea that I felt would put more money into my pocket, teaming up with one of my colleagues from the firm. I told my plan to Sara since I always wanted to keep her in the loop with what I was doing with our money. Even though I was the one making 95 percent of the money, I had no problem with that because I've always dreamed of being able to bless my wife with the option to stay home and raise our kids. My father loved and loves my mother dearly, but unfortunately, my mother had to work extremely hard her entire life. I aimed to make sure my wife could do what she wanted to do, and with my position at the law firm, I was able to do that with ease. Sara's passion was to teach Sunday school, so I wanted to give her all the support necessary for her to be able to pursue that. A close colleague of mine at the firm named Bob talked to me about splitting our commissions differently so that we would get them more consistently. The lawyers at the firm agreed with our idea as well.

Sara was nervous about the idea, but I felt secure that I had all the information I needed to move forward with it. Sara said that she was going to ask her parents' opinion about how I should split my commissions. I said to Sara, "With all due respect, I don't care what your parents' opinion is about the way I split my commissions or spend my money." I told Sara that we are our own family, and that we don't have to consult with her parents every time I want to buy a pair of pants. Even though Jim was a mentor to me for business, there were still things I wanted to do on my own. Even though Sara's intentions may have been good, I was actually really offended that she brought her parents up like that. It made me feel like she didn't trust my business sense. I did understand that her dad was a great businessman in the city, but I was clearly making my own waves in the business world as well. I told Sara I don't want us to talk about this situation with her parents, and we agreed that we would not.

Two days later, Sara's mom, Tiff, and I were hanging out, and she said something that caught my attention. She was saying specific words that I had only said to Sara about the deal I was doing with my colleague at the firm. The mom tried to give me advice in an indirect way, but her cover was already blown. I told Tiff that I was going to catch up with her later. I immediately called Sara and demanded that we meet as soon as possible. We met at her lake home and got right to the point. I said, "Why would you tell your mom after you already told me that you wouldn't? Do you just lie about everything?" Sara instantly started crying and said, "My mom is so dumb. I told her not to tell you." I just looked at Sara in disappointment, saying, "I don't even know you right now. How am I supposed to trust you if you keep lying about everything?" I left the lake house to head to a client meeting, and when I got out of the meeting, I had a message from Jim on my phone, saying that he would like to talk.

I drove to Jim's house, but it was only Jim and Tiff there sitting on the couch like someone had died. I walked in, and Jim asked me to take a seat. I sat down, and Jim said, "Leonardo, this kills me to tell you this, but Sara wants some time to think about the marriage. I don't think it would be good for you two to stay in the same house while she makes up her mind. She is staying at her friend's house tonight, and I'm going to ask you to move out by tomorrow night. We are telling everyone that the wedding is off." Jim then hands me back the ring in the box I gave it to her in. To say that I was absolutely and utterly crushed would be a gross understatement. The feelings of disrespect, anger, sadness, and abandonment swarmed my heart. I grabbed the ring and just drove around for hours that night, trying to clear my mind. I really couldn't believe that Sara and I just went from arguing about her lying to me being broken up with, by her dad. That should have been the second time that I ran for the hills, but I didn't.

The next morning, I came to Sara's parents' house early to get my stuff and move into my apartment early. As I was packing up, Tiff said, "Leonardo, just know that this is hard for us too." I just laughed and kept packing. I took all my stuff to my new apartment and dumped it on the ground. My furniture had not arrived yet since the landlord let me move in early. No bed, no TV, no finance and nobody but me. I just sat in this big apartment, staring at the wall, trying to figure out my next moves. I tried to figure out if I would stay in Chicago if Sara and I did not get back together or if I would move back to Jersey. I called Sara several times but only got her answering machine. I texted her and got no replies. I called out of work two days so I could figure things out with my situation. I couldn't even sleep. On the second day that I was off, Sara called me. She told me how much she missed me and was crying, asking to see me. I told her that I was at the apartment, and she sped over. I heard the knock on the door, and then Sara ran in and jumped in my arms. She wrapped her legs around me and started kissing me like crazy. I was confused at what changed in her mind, but in that little pocket of time, I really didn't care. Even though there were red flags all around this situation, I numbed myself to the pain again. I was just happy to have my Sara back. Even though I probably should have called it quits by then, I still saw the good in Sara, and I was willing to overlook these shortcomings.

Sara and I sat on the floor and talked for hours about what we needed to do to communicate better and rebuild our trust. Sara and I were sure that we wanted to be together, but we now had to convince her parents of that. The next day, I called a meeting with Sara and her parents. I told her parents that we loved each other and were going to make it work no matter what. Jim said, "Leo, I love the way that you came back to fight for my daughter. That's the kind of man I want my daughter to marry! You have our blessing to get married." Since we cancelled the first wedding date, we had to find the next closest opening. The original wedding date was October 16, so now we had to push it to November 29. New wedding invites were sent out, and the wedding was back on! I thought that nothing else could go wrong before we got married, but we weren't out of the woods just yet.

One morning at breakfast, Sara and her sister got into a huge fight over something random, but then Maria said something about Sara being the town hoe. My ears perked up because I was curious as to why her sister would even jokingly say that about Sara. When Sara and I had some alone time that day, I brought up their argument from earlier. I asked Sara why her sister would call her the town hoe. Sara explained that she would constantly get accused for stealing other girl's boyfriends. I asked Sara if it was true, and she quickly said no. Now when I first started talking to Sara, the topic of boyfriends came up, and she told me she only dated three guys in her whole life. When I asked her during this conversation I was having about her being the town hoe, she now told me she had five boyfriends. One thing about me is that I've got an incredible memory, so I made a mental note of the inconsistencies in her stories.

As time kept getting closer to the wedding, the weirdest things kept happening. It seemed like no matter where we went out together, we were running into her exes. I mean everywhere. There was a time we were getting our car washed, and the guy scrubbing my car looked in my car and yelled, "Sara Smith?" I asked Sara how she knew him, and she told me that was one of her former boyfriends. We were at a wrestling match, and the guy getting slammed looked into the crowd afterward and said, "Sara Smith, is that you?" It was the same situation with that guy being her ex. We were out at dinner one night, and one of the waiters was pointing and laughing in our direction and then yelled Sara's name across the restaurant. By that point, I was ready to knock the guy out in my suit. The same situation with one of her other exes happened in the mall. This kept happening time after time to the point where I almost wanted to stop bringing her out with me. After these situations happened five times, I had a little more peace of mind, assuming that I wouldn't have to worry about running into any more of these guys. I couldn't be mad at her for having exes as she didn't know me back then. I just had to pull the exes to the side any time they yelled her name out in a public place like they owned her. All her exes respected my demands to respect our space. Sara and I got through that, and it made us stronger. We were excited because the wedding was less than a week away. Friends were flying into town. Alterations were still being made to bridesmaids' dresses and the tuxes. Flowers were being delivered, while last-minute decorations were being signed off. All this work, preparation, and planning had come down to this very moment.

It was now the wedding day, the most important day of my life! I opened my eyes and just yelled, "I'm getting married today!" All my best men were sleeping over my house, so they all woke up clapping and yelling too! I couldn't have been more ecstatic, but in the midst of all the excitement, I saw that I have a missed called from my older brother. It was a little hard to make out everything that he was saying, but what I did hear clearly was when he said, "You know I'll always have your back no matter what." All I could think is, "Then where are you right now when I need you most?" I figured maybe my brother and family were going to actually fly in today or maybe they were already in town, ready to surprise me at the church that we are getting married at. I mean, my family did get an invite so it's not impossible for them to be here. I thought that has to be it, because there was no way they would actually miss my wedding. My groomsmen and I got suited up and headed over to the church.

When I got to the church, there were already tons of people there, and I was getting pulled in a million different directions. The photographers finally got a hold of me and started snapping shots like the paparazzi. They were taking pictures with me and my groomsmen, me and Sara's family members, and me and random babies. We did the whole "bride surprise" moment, where I turn around while standing at the altar and had to act surprised that my fiancée was standing behind me. Sara and I also went backstage and signed our marriage certificate, which was terrifying, by the way. It was a very important piece of paper, and I usually forget how to spell my name in those situations. I nailed it though. My best man was talking to me the entire time, getting me jacked up, as a great best man should do! There was also a time when my best man, Mark, called me to the side before we all walked in for the opening ceremony. He said, "All jokes aside, how you are feeling about this? I just want to let you know that if you feel weird about this during any point in the service, tap me, and we will walk out of here together. I'm serious man." I told Mark that I appreciate it, but that I was okay, and then we lined up by the doors. Before the doors opened, I started wondering if Mark was on to something that I wasn't and was trying to indirectly warn me. Either way, there was no turning back now. The doors opened. All the people from the wedding party flooded in. I made my way in, escorted by Sara's mother. I was now waiting at the altar, more nervous than I had ever been. All I kept saying in my head was, "This is it." As I stand there with my one hand over the other the back doors to the church open. Then the "Here Comes the Bride" song came on, and everyone in the church rose up. Sara joined her dad, Jim, at the back of the church, and they made their way toward the altar. Sara and Jim arrived at the handoff point just like we practiced the day before. Jim was just a mess at this point, a big ball of tears and snot. I don't blame him though. I was tearing up a bit myself too. I helped Sara to the top of the altar, and she was just shining. She was so stunning in her white dress! She honestly looked like an angle that went AWOL from heaven. She just looked divine! The service flew by. There were a lot of jokes, laughs, tears, stories and more laughs, but in the midst of all the laughs I couldn't help but keep looking at the door throughout the service. I was still hopeful that my dad and family would come walking in at any second and stop this huge prank that I prayed they were playing. There were over five hundred people at our wedding, and in that sea of people, I never felt so alone in my life. I was so tempted to tap Mark and just walk out, but I couldn't do that to Sara and her family. If I pulled a stunt like that, I would surely lose Sara forever. I felt trapped and surrounded by bad decisions. I just didn't believe that I should feel like a stranger at my own wedding. I just couldn't compute how my family really wasn't there at my wedding. I mean, this wasn't one of the hundreds of soccer games my dad missed. This was *my wedding day*, for Christ's sake.

There was just so much joy and so much anger mixed into that one day for me that I couldn't focus. I zoned out for a good part of the service because I was so hurt. Before you knew it, all I heard was "By the State of Chicago, I now pronounce you man and wife. You may kiss the bride." And just like that, I was a married man! I kissed my new beautiful bride, and we danced our way out of the church. We got in the limo and headed to the reception. Then we had an incredible time at the reception dancing and laughing. The night was getting late, and Sara and I were ready to go to our hotel. We hugged everyone good-bye and I helped Sara into my car, huge dress and all. Please keep in mind that I was still a virgin at this time, so I was slamming on that gas! As I was driving, I also realized that I have no idea what I'm doing when it came to having sex. We arrived at the Sofitel Hotel, where we had our reservation. We got into our room, and she rushed to the bathroom to go put something sexy on. Being the joker that I am, I thought it was a great idea to keep my clothes on and act like I was sleeping on the bed. Sara came out in her lingerie, and I was just acting like I was snoring. She did not find that funny at all. To say the least, we had a great night once I figured which hole to put it in. What? It was dark, and I'm even darker.

We woke up the next morning and headed to her parents' house to open all the wedding gifts that we preregistered for. We had a great time there laughing about all the dances people were doing at the reception, and all the jokes being told during the wedding ceremony. After we opened all the gifts, Sara and I went back to our home. She was not living in the apartment before that time because we did not want to put ourselves in a situation where temptation would be overwhelming. When Sara and I lived at her parents' home, there were always people around in addition to us. I was also working all the time, so it was easy to not mess anything up.

We were now married! We were doing married people things and going where married people go. We now had other married couple friends and were double dating too. Work was still going great, and Sara was teaching Sunday school at her parents' church. I was also occasionally speaking at Jim's two churches, and the congregation really liked it. I also really loved all the children from both churches. Life was just really great for the first couple of months, until we ran into Sara's other ex-boyfriend. It had been a while since Sara and I had that conversation about her being the "town hoe", but the last time we did, she stated that she only had five boyfriends. I asked Sara again when we got alone, but this time, she said she had seven. I called her out right on the spot and pointed out her inconsistency. She started to do the cry that I now know all too well. I gave her no sympathy because she has just been caught in another lie. If it's one thing that I hate, it's when people try to play on my intelligence. I told Sara, "How are we supposed to have a happy marriage if I keep finding out lies every couple of months?" I told Sara to take a day and really think about all the guys she has hooked up with or gone out with because I don't want any more surprises. The next day, she came back to me with the number seventeen. I instantly yelled, "Seventeen? Are you serious? That's a football team! That's a basketball team's starting five, with two substitutes for each player." I was grossed out at first because, up to that time, I had one serious girlfriend in college that I dated for two years and did not have sex with. My focus was never getting girls because I was focused on working and school. My father always told me that there will never be a lack of pretty women, so I always focused on capitalizing on vital but fleeting opportunities. I've had a paranoia of STDs, so I immediately went to go get tested. Results came back, and I was, and am, as clean as a whistle. At the end of the day, even though I was mad that she had hooked up with so many guys, we were married now, and there was nothing I could do.

After getting married, there was an unexpected and ongoing fight that I kept having between Jim and myself. Ironically, it wasn't even over Sara this time though. The fight that I was constantly having was over bad advice Jim gave to my best man, Mark. A few days after my wedding, Mark called me to congratulate me again, but also to confess something. Mark told me how he and one of the bridesmaids hooked up during my reception. I joked with Mark and said, "Bro, that was supposed to be the day that I got some goods, not you." Mark wasn't laughing at all and was dead serious. This was now very serious to me as well because Mark was going out with a very sweet woman that I was also friends with. The fact that he just cheated on her broke my heart. He told me there was more I needed to know. Mark said, "Jim also caught us in the act of hooking up." When Mark told me that Jim saw them, I no longer felt like I needed to make him feel guilty because I was sure Jim would have heavily corrected him. On the contrary though, Mark said he was actually confused on what he should do. I said, "Bro, what is there to be confused about? Just go do what Jim said and confess to your girlfriend." Mark said, "That's the thing, he didn't tell me to do that. Jim said that if he was me, he would wait to confess this bad news to his girl during their fiftieth anniversary celebration." In other words, Jim was telling my best friend not to tell his girlfriend that he cheated on her. I was outraged at the fact that Jim would advise Mark to live a lie the rest of his life. I yelled at Mark for two straight hours, reminding him that we were better men than that, and that we had to be honorable men for our children someday. I ended the conversation by saying, "Mark, you know I love you like a brother, but if you do not tell your girlfriend that you cheated, I will *not* stand next you at your wedding even though you stood by my side at mine. I appreciate you standing with me on my big day, but I refuse to be part of a lie. Tell her, or you can lose my number." I've never had to be that stern on any of my friends, but it just had to be done.

When I told Sara about what her dad said, she didn't seem fazed by it, as if it was normal. I wanted to hear the disappointment in her voice about the disgusting advice Jim gave my friend, but there was none to be found. That alarmed me because it made me wonder if we were on the same page when it came to this issue of confessing our wrongs to one another. This was an important issue to me since I always wanted to have an honest and open marriage.

Jim and I fought for months about the advice he gave Mark. Mark wasn't listening to me, so it got to the point where I cornered Jim at his lake house with his two sons and said, "Jim, the advice you gave was terrible. How can you tell a young man to not be honest with his girlfriend? If your wife cheated on you, wouldn't you want to know?" Jim replied, "No, it would hurt too much. I'm too far invested for me to divorce her now, so I just wouldn't want to know." I turned to Jim and said, "So you are okay with living a lie?" I couldn't believe that he just said that out loud to me with no shame. Then I asked Jim, "So if Sara cheated on me, would you tell me?" Jim looked down, thought for a while, and then put his head up and said something that I never imaged a father would say in reference to his daughter. Jim looked at me and said, "Well, I wouldn't tell her if you cheated on her." In that split second, I lost all respect for Jim or anything else he had to say from that point.

That was the absolute worst answer Jim could have given me at that time because I had already been suspecting that Sara was cheating. A couple months into the marriage, when she was around me, she would just start crying hysterically. She would be crying the same way she cried whenever I would catch her in a lie. She would also randomly start fights with me over nothing and then pack her bags and go "stay" at her parents' house for a night or two. These random fights she would start were happening more frequently as the months went on. I remember one night where things seemed very suspicious. I came home from work one day, and she just blew up on me. The thing that caught my attention was that her overnight bag was already packed and her makeup and hair were done as if she was going out. That was also alarming because we were on great terms that morning before I left for work. I saw that her bag was slightly opened, and in a quick glimpse, I saw some of the lingerie that I had bought her in there. I'm not dumb, so I just made a mental note of why she would need this kind of sexy lingerie to sleep at her parents' house. Her parents only lived seven minutes away, so before she left, I jumped in my car and drove up the road from her parents' house to wait. I wanted see if her car ever actually came. One hour passed. Two hours passed. Three and then four hours passed, and her car never came down her parents' road. They lived on a dead-end road, so there was only one way to get to their house. I called Sara's phone, but no answer. I texted her and got no reply. From that night on, I decided to wear a condom any time we had sex. It was no longer making love at that point because I feel that you can only really truly make love to someone you completely trust. The trust between us was parting quickly before, but completely gone now. The next day, I didn't even bring it up to her when she came back to the house. When she came in to the house, I was still in my clothes from the night before, and she said, "You're up early." I said, "You are too." I went to give her a kiss, and she dodged me, saying that she didn't brush her teeth yet. The funny thing is, I could distinctly smell another type of cologne on her and see a slight bruise on her neck. It was all too obvious that the unforgiveable had been committed. Sara was the type of person you had to catch in the criminal act because she would deny it to the very end, unless you nailed her to the wall with hard facts. I wanted to catch her in the act, but that opportunity would never come for me.

I believe that she knew that I was on to her because the next day, she came in the house literally trying to fight me. I was in the room getting dressed up for work, and she was yelling at the top of her lungs and trying to throw punches at me. I tried to put my hands out to stop her from hitting my face, but she was still able to connect her fist to my face twice. She finally got frustrated that I wasn't raising my voice back or arguing and said, "Hit me, hit me so I can divorce you." I instantly put my hands behind my back and laughed, saying, "Sara, you didn't just think of this, you planned this. You're not smart enough to think of this on your own either, so who put you up to this? Who did? Your mom or your weak-ass dad? Sara, I'm on to you and your family's games, and they're about to come to an end. If you wanted a divorce, why not just ask for one? Why do you need me to hit you for you to get a divorce? Maybe it's because you know that your church will not accept the fact that you just wanted to call it quits for no reason, or maybe there is a reason, like you cheating."

Sara's eyes grew big when I talked about cheating, and that just infuriated her more. She tried to swing at me again, and I maneuvered out of the way. I said, "You know, I always find things out, so you're trying to make your own way out. I already know your dirt, Sara." I saw her coming toward me, getting ready to swing again, so I grabbed my keys and phone while she punched and scratched at my back. I left and got in my car. I called my dad immediately and told him about how Sara just tried to get me to hit her. He told me to get as far away from the house as possible. I never had a female try and put hands on me in my life, so I didn't know what to do in this situation. My dad helped me realize that she was trying to use me as a reason to get a divorce by saying that I was abusive. My dad said, "Leo, you are a strong African American man, and the cops would not think twice about shooting or locking you up in Chicago." He helped me understand the severity of domestic violence and how that can stay on a man's record the rest of his life. That could even affect jobs I would go out for in the future.

I went back to the house later that evening to get some clothes because I knew Sara would not be there. I bought a ticket to Tulsa to go see my old pastor and my best friend, Mark. I explained the situation to Mark when I reached Tulsa, and he commended me on not feeding into Sara's games. I told my pastor in Tulsa and Mark that I would probably have to divorce her if she keeps acting like this because I would not go to jail over a woman who wants me to hit her or be involved with her family's illegal activities.

One thing I found odd about our first months of marriage was how often Sara kept trying to get me to work under Jim in their church. Jim also constantly asked me to take a position directly under him. He tried to sell me on the fact that I would be second in command, and that I would have authority to sign off on important documents. As appealing as it sounded I continuously declined their offers. I just did not see why there was so much pressure on me to take a titled position under Jim. I was already making great money at the firm, and Sara did not have to work besides being a Sunday school teacher. I was also serving in the church in different capacities. I was preaching a couple times a month. I was also singing in their worship group and cleaning the church from time to time. I didn't understand why I needed to be a titled assistant pastor to him. I was fine where I was and was not going to budge.

A couple months into our marriage, I also came across an article that was released about Sara's family members in the *Star Tribune*. It was about her grandfather on her mom's side, uncles, and cousin who had been involved in multimillion-dollar schemes that ripped off and affected hundreds of people in Chicago. Several of these schemes had to do with real estate and fraud. This also started to make sense why some of the people in their church were abruptly leaving. All of a sudden, I remembered back to the time when Sara's family visited my family in Jersey. I was hearing my father's voice talking about how I should do research on Sara's family because something wasn't right. This seemed to be what my parents were talking about. In addition to that, one of Sara's cousins named Megan, which I was very close with, told me about how Maria and she were pulled over in one of the family cars. Megan told me that when the officer asked for the registration, the expensive car was under the church's name. That made me furious because that led me to believe that all the cars and houses were under the church's name, and that the people of the church were paying for this lavish lifestyle without even knowing it.

I didn't want to just jump to conclusions, but things were becoming pretty black-and-white quickly. Then I knew things were wrong when we were all having dinner at the Cheesecake Factory, and Jim mentioned that he would make $275,000 from the churches that year. An alert immediately went off in my head because even though I'm not the best at math, it just didn't seem to make sense how a pastor could make that much off two churches that have a combined membership of under one thousand people. Things just did not add up to me. I knew that there were certain families in the church who were struggling to keep the lights on, while Sara's family had sports cars, boats, and lake homes. For the record, I am not against having nice things—but to me, it's all about the way that a person gains their wealth. Since Jim was so aggressive about getting me to take a role with the church, I felt that I had a right to know how the money was distributed between himself and the church. When I started asking more and more questions, I realized how Jim got increasingly distant from me. Conversations became shorter and ruder between Jim and myself. I ultimately felt like everything was about to come crumbling down, and I believe that Jim knew it too. I wasn't sure where Sara's heart was at during this time, but I sat her down in our home and said, "Sara, this is what I see going on with your family and the IRS. These issues are real life, and they are already looking for your uncles and a couple members from your church as we speak. They can really throw you and the rest of your family in jail. I love your family, but we need to distance ourselves from them so that we don't get in trouble as well. I'm not going down for anyone's greed."

I told her that she needed to make a decision, and quick on what side she wanted to be on.

The next morning I woke up, got ready for work, and kissed Sara good-bye. I just didn't realize I was actually kissing her goodbye for good. In the middle of the day, while I was on the road, I got a call from one of Jim's church members saying that they were sorry to hear the bad news but that they respect my decision. I said, "What decision?" The church member said, "The decision you made to divorce Pastor Jim's daughter. I just got the mass email about it, which has been sent to both churches."

I hung up the phone and called Sara a million times, but I was getting no response. It bothered me so much that I canceled my last meeting of the day and went home. When I got home from work and walked in, half the furniture in the house was gone. All of Sara's clothes and makeup were also gone. Sara also took every single wedding gift that we were given, except the one given to me by one of my best friends/groomsman Brian Davis. On a side note, when I finally got the chance to speak with Sara months later, she said she took all the wedding gifts because it was from all her family and friends anyway since my family didn't show up. At the present time, my home just became a house, and the only thing left from Sara was not from Sara. There was a handwritten note on the counter from her father saying, "Please grant us *OUR* request for a divorce."

The confusion and anger that overtook my heart was unmatched. I literally just remember falling back on the couch, absolutely devastated. I thought to myself, *did her dad just really say "grant us* our *request for a divorce?"* I know that both of them walked down the aisle together, but I promise I only made vows to one of them. I literally felt like I just took a bullet to my brain. I felt like I was just hit by a train. There was just no other way to explain this pain, and I wish she could feel my pain. I just couldn't believe this was happening. I wanted to fight Jim so badly, but then I honestly couldn't even be mad at him for this. This was Sara's choice as well. She had chosen to keep living that life with her family, no matter how wrong and twisted it was.

Before we got to the point where Sara moved out, we were trying to go to marriage counseling. We were going to work on the issues we had, and get advice on them from an unbiased opinion. By this time, Jim had already shown his true colors and proved that he could not be trusted to keep his word either. It was hurtful and scary for me to see that after Sara and I got married, Jim would always immediately take her side, even if she was clearly in the wrong. Tiff always took Sara's side from the beginning, so I already expected that. I can at least appreciate her consistency with being biased toward Sara. Jim on the other hand surprised me by going back on his word. Sara and I were having a very hard time scheduling a meeting with the counselor, especially since I was communicating with her through Jim. Apparently, Sara and her parents went to one counseling session before Sara and I did. I was briefly told by Sara that I needed to now communicate with her through her dad. I don't know what kind of crappy counseling advice that was, but I was willing to play whatever dumb game they wanted in order to try and get Sara back and save our marriage.

I must admit that, at first, I didn't want to get counseling because I just figured that Sara would lie the entire time, making it impossible to make progress. Then my friend from the firm encouraged me to still try it. That's when I started fighting to get into sessions as soon as we could. I felt like the dad already had way too much involvement in our marriage as it was, but now he was allowed to play gatekeeper too. I just hated this whole ugly mess that we had going on.

Like I mentioned, I was fighting hard to get in a counseling session with Sara, but I had to wait for Jim to give me a time and place. I was in our Monday morning meeting at the firm, reporting in my numbers, when I got a text from Jim telling me a time and location to meet with Sara and the counselor. I hadn't seen Sara for over three weeks by this time because we were separated, so I was eager to see her. I quickly reported my numbers to the lawyers and sped out of the firm. I punched the address given to me by Jim in my GPS and took off. I arrived and ran up to the counselor's suite. I signed in with the receptionist, and she told me that he was waiting for me. I ran into the room and introduced myself to the counselor that I will refer to as Dr. Watson. I then looked around the room and saw that my wife was nowhere to be found. I asked Watson where my wife was, and he told me the session was only scheduled for me. I said, "The *only* reason I came here was to see my wife."

I called Jim and put him on speakerphone so Watson could hear our conversation. I asked Jim where Sara was, and he replied, "Oh, she is not coming. The counselor wanted you to have your own session and then bring us all together." The counselor looked at me and shook his head, denying Jim's claims. I said, "Jim, you're lying, and we need to set up another session right now."

We all agreed to meet that Thursday at the same time. I hung up the phone, and Watson said, "I never advised that." I said to Watson, "See, that is what I am dealing with: a bunch of liars."

I left and returned three days later to find Sara and the counselor sitting in his office. The door closed, and I took my seat. Watson said, "I'm glad that we are all here today. Let's start with where the both of you are emotionally right now. Leonardo, how about you go first." I simply said, "I really miss my wife, and I'm here to make things right and work out our issues."

Watson turned to Sara and said, "Okay, and where you are at emotionally, Sara?" With a monotone voice and no emotion, she sharply said, "I'm done, I'm just done and I want a divorce." I did my best to keep my composure, but I honestly felt like I just got shot in the face with a shotgun at point-blank range.

Watson asked, "How does that make you feel, Leo?" In my head I was screaming, *How the FUCK do you think I feel Watson?"* Inside I felt like my heart just got pulled out of my chest. I felt like I had just fallen fifty thousand feet with nothing but the concrete to break my fall. I felt like I was just set on fire and slowly burning at the stake. "This woman used to be my Bonnie, and I was her Clyde. She was my everything, and now I was nothing to her." Just like that, we were done.

Despite how I really felt inside, I actually calmly turned to Watson and said, "Well, I guess it really doesn't matter how I feel anymore, now does it? Her parents obviously told her what to say, and she's just being a puppet to deliver the message. If she wants a divorce, then that's what I'll give her." I looked in Sara's glossed-over eyes, and I swear, she wasn't even there anymore. I could just tell she had moved on already. As a matter of fact, I knew that she had moved on because she wasn't even wearing her ring anymore. She had given up on us, and I felt like her heart already belonged to someone else. It was clear now that I lost her heart, and that some other man had won it. I was racking my brain once again, trying to figure out how we got here.

Even though I didn't want to lose her, my pride got the best of me in that moment. Maybe I should have pleaded one last time and tried to convince her that we could make this work and try and build a family again. I figured everything else was already lost, so I tried to salvage what I could. I slipped off my wedding ring and asked Sara if she would like the ring she bought me back. She said, "No, and just so you know, you're not getting the ring you bought me back either because in the state of Chicago, that is considered a gift. Sorry!" Sara looked me in my eyes, giggled, and grinned as if to say "I won" with her eyes.

I looked at Watson, and he said, "it's it's true, Leo. It is considered a gift." I looked at Sara and just clapped and laughed and said, "You got me, you got me good." Sara asked Watson if she could leave. Watson gave her the okay to go. I got up to leave as well, and Watson asked me to sit. Watson said, "I know you wanted to save the marriage by how bad you have been trying to get in here, but I advise that you let this one go. I've seen this case play out a million times. I usually would advise someone to always keep fighting for their marriage, but this is one of those rare cases where you count your loses and be glad that you made it out with your life."

I thanked Watson for reconfirming that I was making the right choice and left his office. Since Sara and I were really about to get a divorce, I went to my bank and blocked her off all my accounts so she couldn't use my accounts anymore. If we were cutting our ties, then she was going to get cut off from my money. I took her out every week because I loved to be able to bless my wife; and I loved to see her look nice, so I always took her shopping. My dad always did the same for my mother, so I wanted to be able to bless my wife equally. Sara was no longer my wife, so there was no reason to bless her any further. I know she learned really quickly what the real world was like when you don't have a faithful man providing for you.

The next Monday when I got into the law firm, I was being served with divorce papers. Jim addressed the papers to the head lawyer I worked for rather than to me. Jim clearly wanted to try and embarrass me, and he did because now everyone in my firm knew that I was getting divorced. Jim obviously knew my home address, so there was no need to send it to my firm. Jim also called one of the other head lawyers at my firm that he knew and tried to get me fired. Surprisingly, the lawyer stood up for me and said that they didn't even know I was going through a divorce because my performance had been so good lately. I couldn't believe that Jim, the man that I used to look at as a father and spiritual mentor, was now coming for neck. When a person comes after another person's livelihood—that is the ultimate disrespect.

Jim also took it upon himself to send out another letter to the church, trashing me and making his daughter look like an angel. After Jim's letter went out, I got weeks of hate mail and posts on my FB. I was getting threats every other day from some of his members, while some of his other members sympathized with me. Many people in his church told me that they did not believe Jim's story and wanted to hear my side. After I told my side of the story, many members said that my side confirmed assumptions that they already had of Sara's family.

For months, our lawyers went back and forth about the divorce. We all finally agreed on what was to be paid-out and awarded. I remember sitting in front of the first lawyer when I got the papers and how Sara was yelling, "Come on, hurry up and just sign them already!" I looked at the lawyer and said, "Sorry, Sara has another hot date that she is late for, and we can't keep the boys waiting."

I found it funny how Sara was screaming at me to hurry up and sign the papers in the lawyer's office, but then she started crying when we got in the elevator together to leave. I hit the ground floor, and I put my glasses on and walked out of the elevator. While crying, Sara said, "Stop, you don't have anything else to say to me?" I stopped, turned around, and walked toward her. I said, "You asked for this. You want to keep running away in the damn rain, hoping that I'll come chase after you. That shit isn't real, Sara. Life is not a fairy tale. This is real life, and you really hurt a good man. You know that I loved you with everything I had in me. I'd give my air for you, but you were just ungrateful. Good luck finding another good man. I wish you well." I just remember leaving her in the lobby crying, and even though I wanted to go console her, I was just done with all the games.

It wasn't too long after I heard about members from Jim's church going to jail for fraudulent real estate deals. All of a sudden, it all made sense. I was so grateful that I got out in time. I concluded that Jim and Sara wanted me to serve under him so that if the IRS ever came, they would be able to put the blame on me since I'd be signing off on several of the papers. I'm sure that is what happened to the members from his church who got jail time. One of my good friends from the law firm even had to go be a witness to testify against one of Jim's members. It was sad because I knew one of the men from Jim's church who got sentenced, and he had a three-year-old son and a newborn baby girl. It was even sadder because he was the main breadwinner for his home.

Even though I was done with Sara and Jim's church, I still wanted to stay in Chicago. Work was still going extremely well, and my lease wasn't up for a long time. I wanted to give living there a chance. I also couldn't take any more major changes for the rest of that year. I was now on my own in Chicago.

I now looked at life in a whole different way after the divorce was done. When I looked in the mirror, I just felt like I wasn't the same. I was colder. I was numb. In my heart boiled feelings of rage, revenge, and deep sorrow. I no longer cared about the things I once cared about, and I no longer believed in many of the principles that shaped the foundation of my life. I was a good guy who believed the best about people, and that got my fucking face kicked in. I was mad at my dad for not preparing me for this. I was pissed at God because I didn't understand how he could let this happen to me if he really loved me. All I knew was I was feeling pain, and I was going to make everyone feel it with me. I was about to enter the darkest time of my life, and things were about to get ugly, quick. I felt myself slowly drifting away from the light and into the darkness.

# THE DARK SIDE

# Transparency

I'D LIKE TO start by saying, "Don't *ever* say that you'll *never* do something."

Warning Note: I have never said that I was perfect, but I do claim to be the perfect reflection of imperfection. I'll be the first one to admit that I've made some serious mistakes in my life following my divorce, many that occurred during this time period. Several of the things that I confess to in this chapter may cause me lose friends and supporters. Many of the sins I admit to in this section may cause me to lose respect from loved ones and family members as well. I also quite possibly could be jeopardizing my chance to ever fall in love again, seeing that, my past may be unforgivable for some. To each his own. I have counted the cost of what I'm about to do and debated back and forth about even including this chapter in my book. I've decided that if this book saves one marriage or stops one bad marriage from happening, then all the dirty stares and embarrassment will be worth it. The most important part about telling the truth is that you have to tell the *WHOLE* truth. A half-truth is a full lie, and I am not a liar. There is good and bad to us all. I'm just honest enough to show you all sides of me, hoping that it guides people away from the wreck I got myself into. As I mentioned in the beginning, I've already made peace with my demons, so your stones and judgment can no longer hurt me. Always remember that integrity is not about living a perfect life, but it's about being able to confess and admit when you are wrong. I'm not afraid to say I'm afraid sometimes, and that is where the first steps to healing takes place. This is me being transparent in my darkest hour.

After the divorce papers were signed and the attorney fees were paid, I just sat in my car and wept. There were so many mixed emotions and so many unanswered questions that I just felt paralyzed. Out of all the emotions that were erupting in my heart, anger was the most prominent. I was so confused, and I honestly felt like I was drowning in an ocean of anger. First, I was furious at my new ex-wife for all the lies she told me, that I had to find out about. I was mad that I even still loved this woman when I should be hating her. I just kept thinking, how could a woman let a man get on his knee and propose to her when she knew she had secret lies she did not disclose to him? I was upset with the way her family just turned their backs on me at the drop of a dime, and started spreading rumors. I couldn't believe that my now ex-father-in-law had the nerve to call the law firm that I worked for and tried to get me fired. Even though my feelings were misguided at some points, I was still angry at my father for not warning me about this grey area of love that I am currently in. Dad taught me that if I love my wife and protect and provide for her, she will never want to leave me or break my trust. I thought the formula was A + B = C. I had no idea that "B" could be such a wild card variable.

I was mad at God because I couldn't figure out why he would let his son who waited until marriage get blindsided by this devilish diva. I was disgusted at how some of the members from my ex's church treated me after her father sent an e-mail to the church saying that "I am choosing to divorce his daughter." Mind you, this letter was sent while we were separated and still in the process of trying to talk things out. The list for the people I was angry with was a mile long. Out of all the people I was angry with, I was most disappointed in myself. I just couldn't get over the fact that I was twenty-four and divorced. In that moment, there was just so much pain, so much humiliation, and so much darkness.

I was so angry I felt like I was *on fire*. All I saw was red, and everyone was a target. I felt pure hate pumping out of my heart while I felt my emotions going numb. For the first time in my life, I just didn't care what happened. If caring got me here, then I want to do everything opposite of that so that I never had to feel this way again. Sara hurt my pride, but I knew just how to hide all my sorrow and all my pain. I did my *crying in the rain*. I couldn't let Sara's family see me sweat or hurt. So I started posting pictures on Facebook of me going out and having fun like it didn't even bother me. It bothered me more than words can express, but I was also bothered by the response of woman. After I signed the divorce papers I waited about two weeks to change my status on Face Book. Reality sunk in for me after I saw Sara post a picture of her and another guy kissing. I waited until the middle of that night, because I figured that no one would be up, but I was so wrong. The moment I changed my relationship status I was getting flooded with calls, inbox messages, and naked pictures from all kinds of females. I was disgusted that they didn't even want to give me time to heal or time for the blood to dry before they attacked like vultures. There was no sympathy, just selfish intentions on their part.

I want to make it clear that during this time, I did not drink any alcohol or do any drugs, even though there were several nights that temptation would come over me, and I wanted to fill the tub with alcohol and just *dive in*. I remember going to the mall and buying a ton of new expensive clothes, and then just hitting the club *every* night. I was so lonely in this city, and I tried to do whatever I could so that I wasn't at my old condo. My condo reminded me of her too much, and it didn't help that it still smelled of Sara's perfume. Even though I no longer believed in love, I just wanted to feel like it still existed. More than that, I wanted to make other people feel my pain. It's been said that hurt people hurt people, and that saying couldn't be truer. Its evil, but I now wanted to make women fall in love with me the way my ex made me fall for her and just crush their worlds. I doubted that I could ever trust another female again, so the thought of getting married again was not even fathomable.

I remember the first girl I slept with after I was divorced. I felt horrible inside. Thoughts ran through my head of how wrong I was and how I wish I was still with Sara. I was so used to my ex's body that I just couldn't believe that I was inside another woman. I felt so bad about the whole thing I kicked her out and called a cab to take her home. It just felt weird to have another woman in the bed that my wife and I used to lay in. The next time I had sex with another woman, it was great because I truly didn't care anymore. I concluded that I do not want to ever get married again. I figured that if saving myself will not save me from being lied to again, then there is no point in holding back. Plus, Sara had seventeen boyfriends and I partly felt cheated. I was turning down girls left and right my whole life, and Sara was just giving back to the community and letting everyone have a ride like a subway.

It was sick and twisted, but revenge, at that time, was sweet. I was constantly in bars and clubs, getting into fights and just beating the snot out of people because I just wanted everyone to hurt. I just remember always throwing chairs and hitting people with bottles. I would start talking to another guy's girl in the club to purposely get in a fight. After I beat him up, most times his girl would want to leave with me. I would take the new girl home, have sex with her, and then call her a cab. After a while, I stopped paying for cabs for the girls. I just didn't care anymore. I was making great money, so I was blowing money on women and clubs every night. I remember my spending habits being out of control and burning through fifteen thousand dollars in a week. Between the daily VIP bottle service, strip clubs and hotel pent house suite parties I was throwing, money was getting blown fast. Strip clubs became a second home to me, and gave me the false love I needed to stay sane. In the midst of all the money throwing, bottles popping and all the sexy women, there were several times where I would just look around and get infuriated with Sara. I kept saying to myself that I shouldn't be in here. I wish I was at home watching a movie with my wife. I was mad that she had forced me to this lifestyle. Then I shook off those thoughts and kept ordering more bottles and more girls. Keep in mind that I never had to pay for a woman to be around me, I just liked throwing money because it made me feel powerful. These were all just pitiful ways to camouflage my pain. I was just a good man who had given too much to the wrong woman, and had nothing left to give.

I was careless, reckless, and heartless. At this point in my life, I was not at all myself, not even human—more like some sort of animal or beast that feasted on the hearts, hopes, and emotions of others. I was something like a monster. I did so many things that I said I would never do. I've broken hearts, I've wrecked homes, and I've burned bridges with good people. I've been with more women than any three men should be allowed to have in one lifetime. Even though I always used protection, I was still wrong. I was destructive, and my whole life was so sad. The thought of marriage was a joke to me. I mocked it and didn't respect the union. I felt that if I can't find love, then no one will. I was so selfish, but I did not care. Some of my best friends, like Lord Brian Davis, tried to reach out to me and help me during this time, but I was already too far gone. I wanted to be healed from my broken heart and Father Time was just taking too long. I figured that breaking hearts would somehow heal mine, so that's what I aimed to do until I was well again.

One night I was in the club with my boys PARKER and SELFISH, and this lady, who I will refer to as Delilah comes up to me. She started dancing really promiscuously on me. So I'm feeling all over her body while she's grabbing my manhood under the strobe lights. I knew she wanted to have sex by how much she was kissing and feeling me up. I was getting harder while she was biting and kissing on my neck and telling me how wet she was. I said, "Let's get out of here," and she grabbed my hand and started leading me out of the club. Parker grabbed me and pulled me aside and said, "Are you crazy, bro? That lady is married. Look at that huge ring on her finger. I'm all about being reckless, but you don't mess with a marriage, bro." I was so caught in the moment I didn't even realize that I was dancing with a married woman. I thought to myself, *what am I doing?* Then I said to myself, "*Oh yeah, whatever and whoever the hell I want is what I'm doing!*" I pushed my friend off me, grabbed her, and led her out of the club. I had a mission to hurt the world, and she was next on the list. Marriage was a joke to me because forever really wasn't forever. It was all a gimmick because I learned that eternity has a limit.

Delilah came in her girlfriend's car with her friends, so we took mine. She said we could go to her house because her husband was far away on a hunting trip and wouldn't be back for a couple days. On the drive to her house, we started talking about life, and I wanted her to quench my curious thirst about her husband. I asked, "Is this your first time doing something like this behind his back?" She told me that it wasn't. In my mind, I figured that she was doing this because her husband had to be a jerk and treated her like trash. I asked her if he was treating her poorly, and she said, "No, he's actually an incredible guy. He's a head doctor in a hospital. He's really kind, good-looking, and a great father. He also allows me to be a stay-at-home mom for our three beautiful children."

We finally arrived at her home, and my mind was blown at what she just said. I told her that I was confused how her husband can be so great and she can still want to mess around behind his back. She said, "It's simple. I just want to have some fun." I was completely disgusted that a human could think that way, and then I looked at myself and realized I was about to do this with her. She led me on to her property, which was a beautiful home on a private lake. There were several brand-new luxury cars in the driveway. We went in her home, and she led me to the room. On the way to the room, I saw her children's toys, family portraits, and her husband's jacket on the kitchen counter. I felt like I was bipolar in that moment. I was having such a war within myself. One part of me was asking what I was doing there, and the dark side of me was ready to get revenge on the world.

We finally made it to the bedroom, and she started to light candles. The room lights went off, and then her clothes started slowly coming off as well. We laid on the bed and began kissing while she unbuttoned my shirt. She was kissing all over my neck and biting and sucking on my lips. Then she slowly started kissing and licking down my chest. She also started softly kissing down my abs. She was still kissing my stomach while she was caressing my penis through my jeans. She continued to kiss my stomach while undoing my belt and zipper at the same time. I wish that I could tell you all that I pushed her off and ran out of the room, but I did not. As she reached into my briefs to pull my penis out she started kissing the tip of it and jerking me off. She asked me to hold her hair back, so I did. She looked up at me while her tongue went in a circles around my tip, and then she put both hands on my penis as her mouth slowly slid down it until it started going down the back of her throat. While I was deep in her throat she slowly looked up at me to see if I was enjoying it, but it made me uncomfortable for a bit because she had the same colored eyes as Sara.

With a hand full of her hair I kept guiding her head up and down on it as she quietly moaned and gave me oral. Her moans reminded me of Sara's moans as well, so I stopped her and laid her on her back. I put a condom on and started sliding my penis up and down her clitoris. As she moaned and begged for me to put it in I finally slid my tip in and her head whipped back and her body quickly tightened up. As I began to slowly stroke her, the moans became louder and the pitch became higher as she clawed my back and tightly gripped the back of my arms. Every now and then, I would kiss and bite her passionately and I would slide my dick in as deep as she could take it without her crawling up the bed. Her legs were shaking so hard and her eyes were rolled all the way in the back of her head. Her head kept hitting the headboard even though I was grabbing the back of her neck at some points. I pulled all the way out of her and my condom was soaking wet. I turned her over and started to stroke her from the back. I grabbed a handful of her pretty, long hair and pulled it back hard enough to break someone's neck, but she loved it because after a long while she started screaming that she was about to cum over and over as I slapped her ass so hard that it left imprints on her cheeks. I kept stroking deep and hard and then let her hair loose. Delilah whipped all of her hair to one side of her head and looked back at me while I grabbed her by her little waist and kept pounding my dick into her extremely wet, warm vagina. There was just something about the way she looked back at me that reminded me of Sara, and after she had her orgasm I just stopped stroking. The thought of Sara finally sobered me up somehow. I didn't even care to get my orgasm off because my mind was now completely on Sara. Delilah said, "That was amazing!" All I could say was, "I'm sorry, but I have to go now." I went to the bathroom to clean myself off and get dressed. When I was in the bathroom I looked in the mirror and just wanted to break it. I was so ashamed of myself I just sat by the mirror for a while. I had a major lapse in judgment that night, and I had sex with another man's wife. I crossed a man who did absolutely nothing wrong to me. I was becoming everything that I hated. I wasn't making the world better. I was repeating the evil that had been done to me. Delilah wanted me to stay over, but I felt so gross that I just walked out.

When I got in my car, I started it up and took off. The thought of what I just did was already haunting me. When I was a couple of miles away, I pulled over to the side of a gravel road because my heart was so heavy. I looked at myself in my rearview mirror and just started weeping. When I looked at myself in the mirror, I honestly didn't even recognize myself. The old me wouldn't go for this. Subconsciously, I think I personally wanted to see how deep and how dark a person could actually go, and now I knew. I thought finding out how bad someone could be would make me feel more secure, but now I was a hundred times more insecure. I thought that getting revenge would make me happy, but it only dug me deeper into misery. I hated myself so much in that moment. I stayed on the side of the road for over an hour just sobbing with my head on the steering wheel. I couldn't believe that I just did that. I was empty and needed meaning. I made a promise to God that day that I was never, ever going to sleep or even approach another married woman in my life. I have kept my word ever since. Friends, please remember that revenge will never heal your wounds, only time and forgiveness will.

Time would go by and I would flip from being the bad guy to the good guy as I tried to date again. Even though I was in monster mode every now and then, a major sense of conviction would come over me, and I would go to the mirror and look at myself in disbelief. I would say, "I'm going to change." Then I would go out and try and find a good girl, and it would always result in me letting my guard down and the girl eventually showing her true intentions. Then I would be even more furious than the time before, and I would resort right back to breaking hearts. The monster would return fiercer than before, hungry like a starving lion. At that time, it seemed like the only thing that could satisfy that monster's hunger was feeding on the pain of others.

For the next couple years of this, I went through waves of this behavior. I fall for a girl, I get hurt, and then I hurt others over and over. It's was a horrible downward spiral. And every time I would go through this cycle, the monster inside would get bigger, stronger, and harder to get rid of the next time around.

I consistently found it harder and harder to get rid of the monster, because each time I turned back into him, I had so much more evidence that all women just want to play games. It would always be the previous girl who hurt me that became my fuel to destroy the next ten. It got to the point where I would just *love them and leave* them, because I didn't see anything being genuine.

Even while I was doing all this dirt and sleeping around, inside, the hole for love just got deeper and darker. I didn't want to be a player—that's never been me. I just felt like the good guy was always losing, so it shocked me to see how girls begged and ran back to me when I would be a jerk to them. The girls I would buy flowers for and take to dinner would always run off with a bad boy, so I became a bad boy. You know it's bad when all the strippers in the city know your name and have all become your Facebook friends. The strippers loved me and the group of guys I was now running with!

I had met these guys through a mutual connection that heard some of my music. These men all had colorful backgrounds. These men consisted of drug dealers, gangbangers, and killers. The majority of these men were felons in one way or another, but ironically, these men were some of the most genuine and caring people I knew. We linked up because of our love for music, and these men quickly became like big brothers to me. They were my new family, especially since my ex-wife's family disowned me, and my biological family and I were not on speaking terms. Due to the fact my love for music and the way I would break girls' hearts, they renamed me J-Mu the Monster, and the "J" stood for Jekyll. My main goal was to kill and conquer the city with my new felon friend.

One of the guys from the group who I considered a brother was my friend SELFISH. Selfish was hands down the best rapper in the city, but the whole group new that he literally was the best rapper in America. He just wasn't getting the right offers from the labels, and he wasn't going to sell himself short. He along with the rest of this felon family taught me everything about the streets so that I wouldn't get killed in the wrong part of town, or robbed by one of these shady females. They taught me about how much trouble you can get in by being involved in the drug game and other ways to get money when you're down and out. All this was so new to me, but it was preparing me for the storms that were coming!

One of the friends that I met in the group was named Dante, but he said, "You can just call me Parker." He became like an instant twin to me! He was not like the rest at all. He was more far removed from the felon lifestyle after coming back from jail and realizing that he had to be a better man for his infant son. Parker was calm, confident, and very business-minded. He also had a dark side that reminded me of mine. The first time we met, we started finishing each other's sentences within the first two minutes of us ever speaking. That's when I knew this would be my business partner for life. It was weird to say, but that was definitely a God moment/connection. Parker would be very instrumental in my music career because he produced the best beats I ever heard in my life. He also great at writing music and helping me get my feelings on to paper. Hearing Parker's story about how he changed his life for the better made me want to be better as well. After I made up my mind to stop fighting in the clubs, I figured that I had to redirect my energy and anger in a more positive form. Even though we did our best not to start any fights in the clubs, from time to time Parker and I would find ourselves back to back fighting against several different guys because they were mad that their girls liked us. Parker and I didn't want to keep hurting people so we channeled all our energy into making our music. Music seemed to be the best outlet for me to vent and conduct therapy/surgery on myself. It was a way for me to be transparent. Music allowed me throw up all my emotions and then look in the mirror to see what was really going on inside me. At this point in time, music was saving my life. Within the first couple times of Parker and I met, we made a plan to give everything we had into our music careers so that we could live our dreams, take care of our families, and laugh at all those who ever hurt us.

Parker and I moved in together and started running full speed at our music dream. Due to his background, it was hard for him to get a quality job, but his God-given gift for music was unmatched and undeniable. At this point in my career, I was still working for the law firm and making great money. Our plan at that time was for me to make the money, and for him to make music all day until I would come home and collaborate on it with him. If we weren't making music or making money, we were in the club getting women. We had the ultimate bachelor pad in Chicago, so after great nights of clubbing, it was easy to bring girls back to the house and hook up with them. I constantly thought about how my ex told me that she had seventeen boyfriends before we were married, so I often felt like I got the short end of the stick. I felt cheated like she got to have way more fun than me. At this point, I also did not think that I would ever get married again, but if I did, I wanted to make sure that I never felt cheated again.

Parker and I were in the club five nights out of the week sometimes. We always had new girls in the house. We honestly already felt like celebrities because we got so much play. We couldn't imagine what would happen when we really made it big. We were wild, reckless, immature, handsome, charming, talented, and super cocky! The world was ours for the taking, and we were going to take it by storm. We were wild and living fast. We felt unstoppable. I remember being on the dance floor in the middle of a club with over seven hundred people in it, and a girl starts dancing wild on me and grabbing me up. She kept putting her face by my crotch and biting on my zipper, so I tapped Parker and said, "She definitely wants it." I proceeded to pull my penis out on the dance floor, and she started sucking me off in the middle of the dance floor. That was a wild phase of my life that went on for quite some time. Things at the law firm were great, and we had money to blow on girls, clothes, and music!

During this time, I would also fly Parker out to California to have meetings about our music and try and get us a record deal. After about two and a half years of partying and flying Parker all around America for music, he got a call from one of the representatives of a major record label—which I will refer to as KONA, over in California. We flew out to California, and they told Parker that they wanted to sign him. We couldn't have been more excited. We went back to Chicago and packed up our lives, and two weeks after I gave my two-week notice to the law firm, we moved out to California. Our dream was coming true—or, at least, we thought it was.

We got out to LA and moved into our new apartment. The celebrations began immediately when we unpacked and continued on for the next several weeks. We still did not have the deal finalized yet because Parker's manager from the label told us she was going to get him the biggest deal possible. We trusted his manager, whom we will refer to as Karen, to get the deal done soon. We had already spent thousands moving out to LA, and rent was coming up while my savings was depleting from all the partying.

Parker was constantly getting in arguments with Karen about closing the deal; so one day, out of the blue, Karen decided to terminate her contract with us. The only reason we felt that she terminated us was because she had lost the deal by asking for too much money. Chips just hit the fan, and shit got real really quick. We were now in California with rent about to come up, a car note that needed to be paid, and drained savings. When we got the letter of termination, we were at the movies. We drove home and literally had to talk ourselves out of sending a girl to Karen's house to slap her head off. The last time I was this mad was when I found out my ex-wife was lying on me to her family and church. Parker and I prayed so hard that God would take away this anger from our hearts, and he slowly did after some time.

It was like our worst nightmare just came to life. I just gave up my six-figure job at the law firm, and my role had already been filled there, so I couldn't just go back. The only hope we had to survive in LA was the last deal I closed at the firm before I resigned. I had not been paid out on that deal yet, and it was worth fifteen thousand dollars commission to me. But something was slowing down the process of the money being released to me. My friend, Elijah, who also worked at the firm with me, would lend me increments of the money until the whole deal went through.

I had to borrow against my money and pay Elijah back everything, between paying back the firm with interest for borrowing against my money, rent, gas, and food. That fifteen thousand dollars was gone before I really even got to hold it.

Once again, before I knew it all my money was gone. We had no music deal, no job to go back to, and we were already three months behind rent now. Times progressively got harder to survive. Parker and I knew that we had hit rock bottom when we had to go to Burger King and split a cheeseburger because we didn't have enough for each of us. We were also sleeping on air mattresses at this time in our apartment in LA. When I could, I was aggressively looking for a new job because I would rather die than go back to Chicago as a failure. I was connected to a publicist in Beverly Hills, who made me her assistant publicist, but whenever it came time to pay me, she was always late. This went on for three months until I just got pissed and quit. I was learning more and more about how cold and heartless the world could be. At a certain point, Parker and I just realized that it would make more sense for him to go back to Chicago. A friend of ours bought him a ticket back to Chicago, but when he got back, he was homeless and hopping from house to house and couch to couch until his girlfriend Moy took him in. Moy was an absolute savior for us at this time because I did not have the money to hold Parker and myself up anymore. She never even made us feel bad about our situation. Even until this day, Moy is still one of the strongest women I ever met and one of my best friends!

I was now in California alone because my pride would not let me accept the fact that I had failed at my dreams. Days got longer, and my money was becoming shorter. It got to the point where I remember looking for enough coins in my Cadillac so that I could go to McDonald's and get a McChicken with cheese off the dollar menu. On a side not, thank you McDonald's, you saved my life! Times were harder than ever, and my hope was dwindling quickly. I had done a lot of modeling in Chicago, so I tried to find gigs in California but nothing was opening up for me. It seemed like the floodgates of heaven that I have enjoyed all my life have finally dried up. Even my credit cards were maxed out with no time to pay them off. I was months behind on rent and months behind my car payment and student loans. It was easily one of the worst times in my life. I watched my credit score, which I worked so incredibly hard to build, come crashing down. No matter what I tried, I couldn't stop it from happening. I became sadder and more depressed. I even became numb to the point where I just went into animal-survival mode. I remember being in my apartment in California one evening and praying that God would just take my life. I figured I had completely ruined my life, and there was no coming back because I was too far gone. The beautiful life that I was once blessed with had been stripped from me, and I had nobody else to blame.

I remember falling asleep that night with tears rolling down the side of my face, with my fist clenched, seriously hoping for God to have mercy and just end it all. That night, I contemplated ending my life, because I could only see things getting worst for me. I remember trying to figure out if I should use a gun, a knife or a noose. I remember thinking how I wouldn't be mad if God just didn't wake me up the next day. The next morning when I woke up and opened my eyes, I immediately yelled "FUUUUUCCKK" until I ran out of breath. I put the blanket back over my head and went back to sleep for a whole day. It was safe to say that depression officially landed. I woke up the following day remembering a verse my father used to read to me when I was a little boy. It was Proverbs 19:3, which says, "It is a man's own foolishness that ruins their life, yet their heart rages against God." At this point in my life, I had nobody else to blame. It was my own foolishness that got me there, and I had to get out of *this mess I've made.*

For the first time in my life, I had considered robbing someone. I figured if this world is going to be mean and cruel to me, then I will equally be mean to it. All of a sudden, I remembered a 2Pac song where he said, "My stomach hurts so I'm looking for a purse to snatch." I used to think that was so inhuman and barbaric of him to even consider doing that to someone, but then there I was, about to do the exact thing I said I would never do. Just when I was going to do that and then also get into the drug game, Parker's mother called me right at the perfect time and just started to pray for me and lift me up, and then she sent me money. I felt like God really saved me right there because I already decided in my mind to go through with both.

Things still were not much better even after she sent me a little money because I was so far behind on all my payments.

Everyone from Chicago was begging me to leave LA because they thought I was going to die, which I was fine with, to a certain degree.

It was finally time for me to face the music and leave California. I pulled on every favor anyone owed me so I could get enough money together to drive back to Chicago. I packed my car with all the belongings I could fit and made the thirty-plus-hour drive back to Chicago by myself. This pain I felt was unbearable. I drove into the sunset, watching Cali and my dreams disappear in the rearview. I made the drive straight through but occasionally rested for a couple minutes while my gas pumped. If it wasn't for my friend Michelle Benedek talking to me on the phone throughout the night while I drove, I probably would have died. My hopes and heart were destroyed. I just felt like such a failure. I started to wonder if all my best days were behind me, or if someone put a curse on me. I just felt like life couldn't get any worse; but it could, and it would for me.

When I got back to Chicago, things went from bad to worst. On the day I arrived I remember Moy and Carmen saying how skinny I was, but it was because I didn't have enough money to eat every day in California. For about a year in Chicago, I went from couch to couch, to moldy basements with roaches. Every day I was one step away from having to go live in a shelter. I tried to do everything to get back into corporate America, but no doors were opening. I had a great resume, but no opportunities.

One of the most humbling things I had to do was call my friend Eli from the law firm and ask if he had any odd jobs around his house for me to do to get some money. I ended up cleaning his pool and reorganizing his garage. It was just so sad to see that I went from making six figures with Eli to now cleaning his children's kiddie pool. Eli paid me much more than what he should have for the work I was doing, but that only lasted about two weeks. The money quickly got used up on surviving. Another friend told me about giving plasma to make a couple extra dollars to get by. I *HATED* needles, and the needle used to take plasma was so painful and big. Since all I could afford at the time was fast food, my plasma would come out extremely slow. I would end up spending two hours with a huge needle in my vein just to get that twenty-five dollars sometimes. I was just in a really sad place.

Even though my car payment had not been paid for months, I was still using it to get around and sleep in occasionally. One night, I stayed over Parker's mom's house. Her name was Carmen, and she was the best secondary mother a man could ask for at that time. Even when I was broke and was sleeping on her couch, she would wake me up and say, "Good morning, young King Cavalli." Carmen knew me before I lost everything, and she did her best every day to remind me that I was still a great person without all the fancy things I used to have. She helped me understand that the king is still the king when he takes his crown off to sleep at night. That is a lesson that I will never forget. Carmen's home was also the house that I had my mail go to since I had been evicted from my California home. One morning, I woke up early to give plasma, and when I went outside to start my car, there was no car to start. My damn car got repossessed, and I had no money to get it back because I was so far behind on payments. That was the absolute last straw for me. I now had literally lost everything. By that time, I had lost my apartment and all my money, and I even had to sell my wedding ring. I had no place to go and no way to get around. Losing my car hurt me the worst because that black Cadillac CTS was my first car. I had been working since I was thirteen but was only able to buy it for myself when I was twenty-two years old. I had literally been from coast to coast in that car, and now it was gone. I went back in to Carmen's home and said, "Mama, my car is gone." I dropped my head, and she came charging over to embrace me. She already knew what the situation was.

I had to figure out how to get some money, and I had to figure it out fast. I spent days online, researching ways to make a lot of money relatively fast. I came across a research facility in the town that Carmen stayed in. I couldn't believe my eyes, but it said I could get paid ten thousand dollars if I can make it through their entire thirty-nine-day study lockdown. Till this day, I still can't pronounce the name of that research drug that I was given. Carmen was supportive of anything I would ever try, but she yelled at me when I said I wanted to do this. I said, "Mom, it's my only chance to get my life back." She saw how serious I was, and she just walked over to me crying and put her head on my chest. I put my arms around her, and in the strongest and most confident voice I could muster up, I said, "It'll be okay, Ma." She looked up at me while tearing up and, in a quivering voice, said, "But you don't really know that." Carmen reached up and started touching my hair, ears, and arms and said, "But you're so perfect, and you're so brilliant and creative. I just don't want them to ruin my baby." I pulled her in to hug her again and said, "I honestly think that right now, Parker, Moy, Selfish, and you are the only people in the world who care if anything bad happens to me. Everyone else has given up on me." My family and I still weren't talking at this point. Carmen said, "I really do care, Son-Joe, and I'm going to be there to drop you off during registration." I applied to get into the test. I got accepted, and the doctors gave me a start date to arrive. The day came for me to go into the research facility. Carmen dropped me off and prayed that I be protected from any of the side effects.

I went into the research facility feeling fine, but it was horrifying being in there. I got sick several times while taking the medication, but I didn't want to tell the nurses for fear that they would disqualify me and cause me to forfeit the money. Everyone did not make it to the end of the study because some patients broke out in painful rashes or had to be hospitalized for other side effects. I really started getting scared when my vision started going blurry a couple of times while I was locked in. I was so ashamed, and it was driving me crazy to be locked in that facility for so many days. While I was locked in, Parker made a new song called "My Story" featuring one of our female singer friends named Salimah Bryant! Parker e-mailed it to my phone, and the first time I heard it, I just broke down and cried right in my seat during lunchtime. Even though the song was about Parker's life, it related to mine so much because we had both been through so many ups and downs these past couple of years. I probably listened to that song a million times while being in that facility. It's one of the only things that kept me sane and in touch with reality. Somehow I made it to the end of the study and I received my check for ten thousand dollars.

After I left the facility, I immediately bought an old white Trailblazer. An incredible mechanic with a heart of godly-gold named Clyde Mayfield worked on my trailblazer, and made it run like new. I reconnected and started to live with Parker in his new place, because his situation quickly improved while I was locked in the facility. I realized that this was the beginning of my climb back to the top, so I was hungry for any kind of work. The first friend I made in the facility was named Mychael Harris, and he really looked out for me when we left the testing grounds. He introduced me to working some temp jobs for a couple months to keep minimal money coming in. It was hilarious to me that the very first temp-position I ever had was working in a certain hotel downtown. When I walked in, I was confused by how oddly familiar this place was to me. Then I realized that this was the hotel I lost my virginity after my wedding. All I could do is laugh at how life comes back around in a full circle if you don't stop it half way through. These jobs were degrading for me, but I knew I had to be humble if I ever wanted to be a king again. Some days, I would work over eight hours and only come home with a check that was small enough to let me eat that night and put gas in my car for the next day. I remember bumping into an amazing girl who wanted me to take her for sushi, but I was so broke that I had to make an excuse every time she called. I just didn't think she would give me the time of day if she actually knew my situation. Sorry Herrald.

I was hungry to get my old prosperous life back, so I couldn't wait to get the opportunity to make six figures again. I missed how the kids in the neighborhood used to look up to me, how they used to admire my suits and point at my car and argue with each other about how they were going to grow up and have one just like mine. I miss hoping out of my car and giving the kids dollars so they can get ice cream from the ice cream truck. I missed how the elderly people in my neighborhood would tilt their heads to me as if to give me approval for being a great role model and making money the honest way. I missed being able to help people who couldn't pay their bills. I missed being and inspiration and being able to give people hope.

I knew things had to change when the temp service assigned me to be a janitor in an elementary school for a week. I remember cleaning the hall ways of the school one day and almost breaking down because of the way a young boy looked at me. School was being let out for the day, and all the kids were running out to catch the school bus, but there was this one little boy that looked at me and froze in the middle of sprinting out. He took a couple steps closer to me and just looked me right in my eyes. We didn't say a word to one another, we just stood there looking at each other. He was looking at me as if he was thinking, is that what I'm going to be when I grow up, and I just looked at him thinking that I let him down. I was always in the "slow" classes growing up in elementary, and all the kids used to tease me saying that I was only smart enough to be a trash man. That killed my self-esteem as a child, and I only got over it as I became a man. The boy just put his head down and started walking towards the buses, but I caught up to him and started speaking to him. I found out everything about him from his favorite cartoon super hero to what he wanted to be when he grew up. I told him that he could be anything he wanted to be and that he needed to chase his dreams no matter how impossible they seemed. I gave him the little money I had in my pocket and told him that I believe in his dreams. He waved to me when he got on the bus and I saw him showing his friend the couple of dollars I gave him. At that moment I realized that something HAS to change quick, because I never want my son to look at me the way that, that boy Joey did. I didn't know where the opportunity was going to come from, but I just kept praying and believing that some miracle would happen. I even started going back to The Rock Church in Chicago after I met these two incredible pastors that I call J and JW. They are the most loving and most understanding pastors you will ever meet. They helped me get focused mentally and spiritually, and for that, I am forever grateful. They really loved and nurtured me back to health in every way possible. What's ironic about these pastors is that they knew Sara's parents from years ago. They told me that they stopped associating with Sara's parents for the same reasons I did. It was just great to have confirmation that I wasn't crazy and that I did do the right thing. It was just great to see my curved life starting to turn into a full circle.

As I was slowly putting my life back together, my relationship with my family was also being restored. Randomly one night, I saw a job posting on Facebook from an old college friend that was currently in a managerial position over in New York City for an international headhunting firm. I called him and asked him to explain the job to me. After he explained it to me, I told him I wanted in because it was an incredible London-based company, it seemed fun, and I could make a lot of money there. I sent my resume, my dad flew me out, and I had an eight-hour interview when I arrived. They offered me the position the next day, and I moved to New York City the following month. I was more hungry and determined than ever before. This was my second chance at getting my life back.

Around the time that I got the new job offer, I randomly got a call from an old college friend that I haven't spoken to in years named Vashawn Green. He told me God put me on his heart, and after telling him my new situation, he offered to have me stay with him until I found a place! Out of nowhere, everything just started falling into place. When

I finally arrived in New York, I watched my favorite movie *Pursuit of Happyness* starring Will Smith (one of my favorite actors). There is no movie that motivates or speaks to me like it does. It was now the night before I started my new job, and I visited my dad and asked him to pray for me to be successful, because I had never done headhunting before. After my dad put his hand on my shoulder and prayed for me, I felt that I was ready to try and fight for everything that I had lost over the last couple of years.

When I first started work I didn't really have any money, so I had to use my older brother's old suits. I was embarrassed to show up to work every day since my pants were so short because my brother is three inches shorter than me. I used to try and wear really stylish socks to make people think that I purposely had my suits tailored that way. Little by little I was able to buy a new tie here, then a new shirt on another week. Then I'd save up and buy a new suit one month and repeat the process until I had a whole new wardrobe. I was already incredibly intimidated to be working in the Rockefeller Center in NYC, but I was even more nervous because I seemed to be the only African American in an office full of people from London. Despite what my initial thoughts were when I walked in, everyone treated me like family there and it was the best company I ever worked for hands down!

In the first year, I got several promotions, won a company award, and even broke the record for the biggest contract done in the history of our company's New York City branch. I was also able to heavily contribute to our team winning "Contract Team of the Year." Life is now better than ever, and even though I love California, I have returned to the East Coast just like my dad told Sara's parents I would. To top it off, on February 15, 2015, Parker and I had a major celebration in two cities on the same night. On that same day I got to open up a fashion show during New York Fashion Week, which has always been a dream of mine! Parker got his first major song on the radio! A few weeks after he landed his first song on the radio with a major artist, Parker was offered his first official publishing deal with a major record label. This deal was better than the deal we had lost the first time we went out to California. Life had finally come back around as a full circle for us! It had seemed like our pursuit for happiness had been attained. It was just beautiful to see that, as friends, Parker and I had it all, lost it all, and then came back better than ever at the exact same time! I had been working insanely hard in New York, while Parker was making major waves in the music industry in California.

I feel nothing short of invincible after being divorced, losing it all and then climbing back up the social ladder and flourishing in one of the hardest cities to make it! Some nights I go on the highest rooftops in Manhattan, overlooking the city, and just reflect on what I've been through these past couple of years. Even though there were many nights where I just wanted to die, I'm so glad that I never gave up. Friends, I want you to understand that rainy days don't last forever, and even the dark side has a bright side if you are transparent with yourself and keep your head up!

# RED FLAGS

I ENTITLED THIS CHAPTER "Red Flags" because red flags are used to indicate a sign of danger. Up to the point of my divorce, I could say that, to a certain degree, my life was picture-perfect. The reason why things in my life always worked out so well was because I felt that I was great at identifying danger in the distance and avoiding it at all cost. After the divorce, sleep was almost nonexistent for the next several months. Whenever I was able to gain a couple consistent hours of sleep, it would be abruptly interrupted by nightmares and cold sweats. I would wake up over and over as if this was a bad dream that kept reoccurring every night. I was constantly mourning through the night. For the longest time, I just could not come to terms with the fact that she was really gone, and that I was really lying here in bed, alone and divorced.

Over and over as I stayed up through the nights, I would try and figure how I possibly could have let this happen in my life. Through the next couple months and even years, I really took some time to analyze my full situation and see where I went wrong. I wanted to detect what signs of danger (red flags) I ignored. In my time of reflection and transparency, I recognized that I had completely overlooked specific signs that should have kept me from even marrying Sara. Before I go into my list of red flags that I overlooked, I wanted to state the trite saying, "Love is a drug." It is actually scientifically proven that when people feel the emotion of love, they have heightened volumes of the hormones oxytocin and dopamine.

Dr. Helen Fisher once did a study on newly love-struck couples who had their brains examined and discovered they had high levels of the neurotransmitter dopamine. This hormone stimulates desire and reward by triggering an intense rush of pleasure. At heightened levels, it has the same effect on the brain as taking cocaine. I bring up these points to support the claim that, to a certain degree, love *is* a drug, and many people that are jumping over the broom are under the influence.

I say all that to say that I was deeply in love with Sara and was not in my sober, logical-thinking mind-set. The judgment mind-set that has helped me avoid similar situations like this in the past was now clouded. Ellen Berscheid, a leading researcher on the psychology of love says, "Newly smitten lovers often idealize their partner, magnifying their virtues and explaining away their flaws." Based on Ellen's research, it is easy to see why people stay in unhealthy relationships when it is clear to everyone else that it is not going to work out.

The list of red flags I overlooked in my personal situation are beyond infinity, but here are ten major red flags everyone should try to avoid.

Do your best to *avoid* marrying people who are the following:

1. *Have a problem with telling the truth.* This is a red flag because if an individual keeps lying, trust will be lost. A lack of trust breeds paranoia and insecurities in other partners. If I would have been paying attention to these signs, I should have not married Sara just off the fact that I consistently caught her in lies. I just kept hoping that things would get better, but they never did.

2. *Have a problem controlling their alcohol or substance intake.* You never want to be married to someone who is indirectly dependent on a substance for them to have to "be themselves." If you notice this and confront your partner, but they can't leave it alone, then I advise you to leave them alone. If your partner loved you more than this substance, they would be doing everything possible to overcome this hurdle in order to keep you in their life. You also want to address this early on in a relationship, because this is not a habit you want children being raised around. Keep your future in mind at all times.

3. *Have explosive anger problems.* People who have explosive angers usually lack the quality of being patient. Patience is needed to have a successful marriage because neither partner will do everything right at first, or even ever. My parents who have the best relationship I have ever seen still need to have patience with one another forty years into their marriage.

4. *Have problems controlling their spending.* I advise everyone to avoid these types of people because finances are one of the leading causes for divorce. You don't want to keep working insane hours so that your mate can spend it as quickly as you

make it. Partners must be in agreement about the way resources are used. I have a friend who was doing well for herself and her son financially, but the man she is now engaged with has put her in debt equating to over seven-thousand-dollars. She told me she has never had that much debt, and her savings were never as low as they were until she met him. I believe that, at this moment, she is ignoring a major red flag. I hope she is either able to help her man correct these bad habits, or I hope she is strong enough to move on. I've seen a lot of good people get into bad situations because they feel that they have already invested too much into their relationship. I want to say that it's okay to lose your initial investment in someone in order to save your life.

5. *Have a problem consistently keeping their word.* As partners are building a life together, it is important to have someone who has your back and your best interest at heart. You want to make sure that if your partner says they will be there, that they will actually be there. If your partner says they will do something, then they need to follow through. Talk is cheap, but the right actions are priceless. One key to having a successful marriage is for partners to be able to give each other peace of mind. No person wants to worry if their partner is actually going to do what they said in any scenario. Your word should be your bond, and your bond should be strong.

6. *Have out-of-control eating habits.* Some people enjoy being with partners who are slightly thicker, but it's hard to touch on such a touchy subject. You need to sit down with your partner and have the hard talk of how much is too much; otherwise, you will be on a slippery slope since nothing was established from the beginning. If a partner starts getting out of control with their eating, it may be your fault for not working together in the beginning to set those ground rules.

7. *Consistently talks down to you or others.* Everyone deserves to be talked to with respect. If your partner puts you down in any way that needs to be addressed before vows are exchanged. If your partner cannot stop doing these action, then action on your part needs to be taken to show that you are serious about leaving. Friends, please take time to find partners that show appreciation for who you are. You are valuable, and you deserve to be valued.

8.  *Wants you to cut off your family and friends for no reason.* It is not healthy to have a partner who *only* wants you to be around them all the time. That's selfish, immature, and insecure. There are certain connections and feelings that only come from being around your family that your husband or wife simply cannot provide. However, the role that you have vowed to play needs to be executed by you with excellence so that your partner doesn't have to try and have someone else satisfy the needs that you are supposed to be taking care of. Being able to spend time with your family and friends apart from your spouse/partner allows you to have a healthy and balanced life. A partner who desires for you to be at your best will lovingly encourage this time apart. It will make your partner appreciate the time they spend with you that much more. However, clear guidelines need to be set so that offensive moves aren't made. This is why I was okay with my ex-wife hanging with a group of guy friends or her family. Unfortunately, she wanted to go against the guideline that we agreed upon. At the end of the day, I want all couples, married and engaged, to aim for a healthy, balanced social life.

9.  *Argue over everything.* If you are partnered with a person who has a short fuse, you will most likely have a miserable life. You may start agreeing with things that you truly don't believe in just to avoid a fight. Some people are peacekeepers, and the worst thing for a peacekeeper to do is be joined with a war starter. They will ultimately mix together as well as water and oil. In addition to that, no one wants to always be walking on egg shells to avoid a meaningless quarrel. Make love, and not war.

10. *Hold grudges for long periods of time.* Life is not too short, but it's not long enough for a person to waste days and weeks being mad at the partner they are supposed to love. Address issues as they come up, and then move on.

# COULD WE HAVE SAVED IT?

FOR THE FIRST two years, I literally asked myself that question every night before I went to sleep. I asked that question every time I walked into a restaurant, and the hostess would ask me if I was expecting anyone. I would ask myself that question any time I would see a happy young or elderly couple. I'd even ask myself that any time I would see a pregnant woman, or young child playing catch with their dad in the park. I would just think about how that could have been me, and how that could have been us. I especially thought of it anytime I came home from work, and there was no one there. I even missed some really important weddings of my friends because I was too much of coward to sit through the services. I would just make an excuse of why I couldn't come, and then send them a gift in the mail. I know that's selfish, but the divorce honestly damaged me that bad, and the wounds still felt fresh.

Every time that thought would cross my mind, I had to train myself to remember the pain and humiliation that she and her family put me through. So in actuality, I came to realize that I don't miss her, but I miss having someone to love and grow with. Due to the fact that she feared her father and he had complete control over her, there was no way to ever make it work. The father controlled the whole family and church with his money, which he would threaten to take away if they did not listen to him. I believe Jim and I butted heads so often because he couldn't control me. I made my own money, completely independent of him, and he didn't know how to make me do what he wanted. Sara was possessed by her father, and it ultimately was never going to work. I was never going to bow down to her father, and he was never going to let up. This is what happens when an unstoppable force meets an immovable object. As long as Jim had a say in our life, which was always, we could not have saved it.

There was one situation in particular where I realized how much control Jim really had over Sara. One day, before the time Sara and I were engaged, we were in the mall because she wanted to look at jewelry displays. We stopped at this one special jewelry store. We split up in the store. I was looking at new watches and Sara was looking at bracelets when, all of a sudden, I hear a woman screaming in the store, "Oh my god, I love this so much!" Somehow, my fiancée found her way over to the wedding ring section, again. (Surprise!) I walked over and said, "Is everything okay, babe?" With tears running down her face, she looked at me and showed me another wedding ring. In my head, I was thinking, *is she crazy? Does she think she is going to get a ring for each finger on her hand?*

Sara said, "I love this ring so much more than the other one I picked. Will you be mad if I switch?" I asked Sara if she could hand me the ring so that I could see the clarity of the diamonds, but what I really wanted to do was find that dang price tag before I was selling my kidney to pay this ring off. I found the price tag, and to my surprise, the ring was one-third of the cost of the ten-thousand-dollar ring she originally wanted. Before Sara could say another word, I kissed her and yelled, "We will take it. Please write down all the information for that ring!"

While the saleswoman wrote down the reference information, I pulled out my phone, started recording, and said, "Now, Sara, tell the camera how much you love your new ring." Sara went on and on for about a minute on how beautiful it was and how much more she liked it than the first one she chose. I'm not sure what made me think of recording her, but subconsciously, I think I knew I was getting evidence to prepare for a future fight.

When we got to her parents' home, I went to my room to change. Sara ran to her parents to show them pictures she took of the new ring. Later on that night, when Sara and I were watching a movie alone, she randomly started crying, and I asked her what's wrong. She told me how her dad thought the ring was ugly and that he wanted her to get the other—more expensive—ring.

The word *furious* does not even begin to explain what I felt at that time. I pulled out my phone and played her the recording I made of her at the jeweler. She said, "I know, I know, but now I want to change it back." I told her that her dad had way too much control over her, and I was not going to live my life based on what he likes. I said, "What if I buy us a house, and then your dad says he doesn't like it? Are we then going to pull our offer and lose a house?" She said I was overreacting, but I needed to figure out where it would end with her dad's opinion being more valuable than our own, in our relationship. I should have known that was only going to be the beginning.

Even though we couldn't have saved the marriage under those conditions, I still feel that there were things we both could have done better. When the divorce was complete, feelings of anger and regret filled my heart. I understand that no one is perfect, and I'll be the first one to admit that I made mistakes during our marriage.

One of the biggest mistakes I made during our marriage was letting arguments go on for too long.

There is a verse in the Bible my dad used to quote to me from Ephesians 4:26 that simply says, "Do not let the sun go down while you are still angry, for anger gives a foothold to the devil." To me this verse is saying that a couple should resolve their issues on the day it happens; otherwise, it is so much easier to stay angry and separated the next day, and so on. That's exactly what happened. We would get in a fight, and then she would go storming off to her parents' home, and the first couple of months I would immediately go over there and smooth things out with her. After a couple months of that, I got fed up because I felt like she thought this was a game. Then when she would run off again, I wouldn't even chase her. Sara's mom would call me and say, "Well, aren't you going to come get her?" I would reply, "Sara knows where she lives, and if she wants to be here, then she'll come home. Jim and you aren't helping these circumstances at all. You need to tell her to come back home and figure it out." As the man of the household, I should have been less passive and addressed these issues when they came up so that we could have kept more peace in our home.

To be completely honest, I know that sometimes I had a problem with pride as well, and I'm not proud of that. There were times where Sara and I would argue, and I would have no problem apologizing if I saw that I was the one at fault. Then there were other times where I felt like I'm not the only one at fault, so I'm not apologizing first. That was just immaturity at its finest on my part. Maybe I should have run after her more during times where Sara would storm out of the house to go stay with her parents. Who knows? What I do know is that it was incredibly hard to fight for someone you weren't sure wanted to be with you. I never thought of myself as a loser, so if a person didn't see the value in being around me, then they were free to leave. I felt like her running to her parents' house was an insult toward me. I also felt like sometimes it was good for us to have our space. It was, altogether, a hard situation to find the perfect balance to. I battled with finding a happy medium of wanting to still show her I cared, but not letting her feel like she had control of me. I wanted to be compassionate, but not a doormat. When I was a child, I watched my one friend threaten his parents with running away, and all of a sudden, he got more toys and got to stay out later. I even witnessed him cursing his parents out sometimes and his parents listening to him. I tried that with my parents, and it was an epic fail. I lasted about thirteen hours on my own, and then when I got home after the street lights came on, I got the whooping of a lifetime. Looking back at that situation now, I appreciate my parents' tough love because I'm a strong man, while my young friend is now in prison. At the end of the day, I just wanted to have a peaceful life with Sara, but I can't deny that I contributed a hand to starting the war that ultimately tore us apart

Apart from the countless lies I caught Sara in, the thing that really irritated me was that she continually compared me to her dad and put him above me. As mentioned before, I respected and honored Jim until he started disrespectfully challenging me as a man. Please understand that I adore women that adore their fathers. It's beautiful and great, in its own place. I believe that women also need to have a balance in their life where they transition a lot of their trust from their father to their husband. A woman would not be married to a man if she did not trust him, so trust him! Now if a husband has a track record of constantly messing things up and is stubborn, then you can talk that subject matter out together. As for me, I had made transitions and major life changes flawlessly out of college, so the constant nagging of how Sara's dad did things was insulting. I always tried to help Sara understand we were starting our own family, and that even though we both had our own family way of doing things, we were also allowed to create new ways together as well. That was supposed to be a big part of the fun in starting our own family and family traditions, but instead, it just led to arguments. To put it simply, fathers and husbands should have their own special place in a woman's heart. No husband wants to feel like he is contesting with his wife's father for her heart.

I applaud the women who hold their fathers in high esteem, but don't let that eclipse the good deeds that your husband may be trying to do. For the most part, he might be new at this marriage thing too.

Husbands need support and encouragement in order to do the right things for their wives. If you keep on downgrading his efforts, they will progressively decrease until they halt altogether. Men, if you meet a woman who thinks her father is God, then try and come to a common ground with her and help her understand that you are doing your best. If she continues to be ungrateful for your efforts, then I advise you to gracefully bow out before you make vows to her. That battle is rarely ever won after the marriage is official.

To the ladies, I advise you to do the same if you have a partner that seems to be a mama's boy. Men, no woman wants to constantly be compared to your mother. Making suggestions from time to time are fine, but also be sensitive to the fact that being a wife is no easy task, even if she is a stay at home wife. All the new responsibilities a woman has to take on as a wife can be quite intimidating at first. It may even take her a couple months for her to get into her groove of juggling this new life of duties. Men, I challenge you all to be more supportive and patient. Also, as she is coming into her own as a wife, shower her with words of encouragement and gifts that you appreciate all she is doing. Those words go a long way and will help her feel more confident. Make your partner feel like a winner!

Like I said before, I constantly thought of how we could have saved our marriage for the first two years until I got a special phone call from Sara. Now after the divorce, I was getting calls from Sara every three to four months. The first couple of times, she would just call me to cry her eyes out, and I would just listen. She told me that she felt bad about how everything happened and said she hated her dad for pushing her to get a divorce. She would tell me how bad guys were treating her and how much she missed me. During other phone calls, she would be trying to accuse me of cheating. I would laugh at her and say, "You're so pitiful. You know that you feel guilty for leaving, and now you need to try and justify it to yourself so that you can sleep at night. Shame on you, Sara. Own your mistake. Good luck finding another man who wants to give you the life I did, when most men twice my age don't even want to claim a woman on a social media site anymore. You're a joke." As I started getting over Sara, the calls from her kept coming. Sometimes she would call me and be normal, but other times, she would call crying, talking about how if we had a son he would be three years old right now if we were still together. I would just reply saying, "Sara, you're being really crazy and weird right now, so please stop."

One night I got a call from Sara, and she was asking to meet up. I still missed her a bit, so I agreed to meet up. I hadn't seen her in what seemed like forever, even though it had only been a couple months after the divorce was finalized. She parked up the street from the condo we used to share and told me she arrived. I throw on a shirt and some cologne and walk out. I walked up to her car as she got out, and we gave each other a big hug. She said, "You still smell good," and I said, "You still look good." We got in her car and caught up on life. She told me about her job and her new boyfriend that she loves so much. I shared details about my job and how being single sucks. We laughed, we reminisced, and we even play fought in the car, which led to kissing and, finally, her giving me oral sex in her car. She was awkwardly calm about the whole situation. She told me that she would kill me if I told anyone about this. I told her not to worry and hugged her good-night. As I was walking home, I realized that she just cheated on the boyfriend that she just told me she "loves so much." If she did this to her boyfriend now, who knows how many times she did the same thing to me.

I never talked to Sara after that day. However, a couple months after that last encounter with Sara, her old best friend Kelly reached out to me on Facebook. Come to find out, Sara was now going out with Kelly's brother, and it was tearing Kelly's family apart. What I found to be ironic was how Sara was trying to hook Kelly's brother up with her sister, Maria, when we were still married. Obviously, Sara was attracted to him too. Kelly originally hated me during the time of Sara and my divorce and wouldn't trust anything I said about how Sara played games and was disloyal. Kelly messaged me on Facebook, asking me to make Sara stop. Kelly told me that Sara just kept playing games with her brother's heart, and it was driving him crazy. As sad as I was to hear about Kelly's brother, it also gave me so much peace in my heart. I now knew that I had made the absolute best decision by not trying to save things with Sara like Doctor Watson said. Now I knew for a fact that she was a lying, cheating manipulator. I'm glad that I never spoke to Sara again after she cheated with me because she wasn't even worth my time anymore. To answer the question that I asked myself consistently for two years, the answer is NO, we could not have saved it.

# LOVE LESSONS LEARNED

AFTER AN INDIVIDUAL goes through a traumatic experience, they are usually more aware of it in their everyday surroundings afterward. This is what happened to me in reference to my divorce. Once the divorce was complete, I started encountering an overwhelming amount of young and elderly people who were also divorced. Many people had very similar stories, while others had stories that were way more bizarre than mine. I was also blessed enough to meet a handful of incredible people that had very happy and successful marriages. These people gave me hope to still believe that there is true love out there, and that I should not give up even though I had a horrible experience. Together, these people became my inspiration to write this book. I've learned so many great lessons from both groups of people, and I hope that these instructions impact your life in a positive way, like they have for mine.

The top lessons that I learned about marriage are as follows:

1. Above all love lessons that can be learned, I believe that knowing what love actually consists of is key. An ancient book of wisdom entitled *The Bible* said in 1Corinthian13:4-7 that, "Love is patient, love is kind. It does not envy, it does not boast and it is not proud. It does not dishonor others. It is not self-seeking, or easily angered. Love keeps no records of wrongs. Love does not delight in evil, but rejoices with the truth. It always protects, always trusts, always hopes, and always perseveres." No matter whether you believe in The Bible or not, I think that we all can agree that those words are of sound wisdom for any couple that wants to maintain a healthy and loving relationship.

2. *Agree to disagree.* My pastor and his wife, who are from Chicago, have one of the strongest marriages I have ever witnessed. They have been through everything a marriage can go through within twenty-five years. They told me that in all their years of marriage, one of the greatest lessons they have learned about keeping peace

in their home is mastering the art of disagreeing. Friends, please remember that you and your spouse don't always have to agree on every single subject. You are both still individuals at the end of the day. If you both don't agree on something, make sure to have a neutral third-party person who you both agree can help you and your partner come to a common ground.

3. *Have a healthy sex life.* This lesson was also given to me by my Chicago pastors. Maybe it's my immaturity, but it was awkward talking about my pastor's sex life with my pastors. I laughed the entire time. It was a joke to me, but it clearly was not a joke to them. They told me about how to keep it spicy in the bedroom and changing it up with costumes and role-playing. I won't go into any further detail how my pastor dresses up like Tarzan for his wife, but I will mention that they told me how much effort they put into looking good for each other. They still want to be incredibly attracted to each other. They touched on the topics of constantly dressing nice, smelling good, and being in the best shape possible for one another! They said, "If we aren't looking our best for one another that is honestly, indirect disrespect to our partner." Wives, your husband should not have to ask you to put perfume on or do your hair. Husbands, your wife should not have to tell you to go to the gym and vice versa. Not taking care of yourself puts your partner in an uncomfortable situation. Now, you may have created an unhappy partner who doesn't want to offend you, but it may start other fights out of frustration, stemming from this root problem. Friends, do your best to always be your best.

4. *Make your partner a priority.* A married couple that is very dear to my life talked about how difficult marriage was in the first couple years because they barely spent any time together. Communication and peace in their home grew by leaps and bounds when they decided to make each other a priority in each other's lives. They put each other over friends, colleagues, careers and even family members. They were the number one priority in each other's lives, and they both agree that making that single decision saved their marriage.

5. *It is okay to quit.* If you are a reader that is currently in the process of going through a divorce, I want you to fight with all

your might to make it work. If you and your partner both still love each other even a tiny bit, and you haven't exhausted all possible options to make it work, then I want you to do that before you do call it quits. The reason I named this section "It is okay to quit" is because I want any pre-married (engaged/courting) couples to understand that it really is okay to call it quits before marriage. If a person is in a relationship and sees that their partner is absolutely not the one for them, then it is okay to call it quits. I know that sometimes there can be a lot of pressure from family and friends to marry the one you are with, but it's your life at the end of the day. Don't just keep going with the flow because your partner and you look cute together, or because you grew up together. Don't even do it because your family loves your partner or because this was the first person you ever had sex with. If you are going to marry someone, make sure that it is someone that YOU are madly in love with, and is a great fit for YOUR life.

I personally have always taken pride in the fact that I never gave up on anything in my life. If I committed to something, I was taught to follow it all the way through the end no matter what. That is why, even when I saw so many red flags during my engagement stage with Sara, I kept pushing forward. I should have been more honest with myself and realized that her lies were already killing me and making me more insecure about our love each day. For some odd reason, I felt like all the insecurities and pain would disappear once we were married, but it honestly just intensified them. I tried to cover the wounds, but it felt like the equivalent of getting shot in my leg and then trying to run a marathon. Friends, marriage *is* a marathon, and no wise athlete would attempt to run one right after dealing with a major injury. I did not give myself adequate time to properly heal before I wanted to get back on the racetrack. If I would have realized this one lesson earlier, I potentially could have stopped hundreds of people from being hurt, and maybe Sara and I would still be friends. I, Leonardo Cavalli, take full responsibility for this mistake, and I have truly learned my lesson.

6. *Take care of yourself.* After my divorce, I met a businessman named Richard Mattox, whom I now consider a father figure. He is one of the most genuine men you will ever meet. During the time when I met him, I was very lost after my divorce, so he took me on a business trip over to Laos to speak to their government officials about mining their land for them. While I was there I did a lot of soul-searching for myself. Richard had also been through a divorce before and as we looked out of our hotel balcony toward Thailand, he would give me much needed wisdom on my situation. After he heard my life story, he pointed out that I was always taking care of everyone else. He advised me to take care of myself for once. He said, "You can't be your best for others, especially your future wife, if you don't first take care of yourself properly, physically and spiritually." Those words still reign true in my heart and have

7. saved me from investing too deeply in relationships where I was giving too much of myself without any reciprocation. I often hear of relationships where one partner has a dominating dream, and they expect their partner to just continuously support them. That is very one-sided and unfair. Friends, please be mindful of your mates, and understand that they too have equally important dreams that require your unwavering support. Friends, please learn to give to yourself as you also give to others.

8. *Don't Compare.* I was recently introduced to a man named Kevin Orellana by my good friend Justin Greathouse'. Kevin and I quickly became friends as I took interest in his incredible photography skills, and he took interest in my music. I came to realize that Kevin was actually married at twenty-three years old as well, but was married for three years at this point. He mentioned that one thing that has kept him and his wife strong is staying focused on their family only. Kevin mentioned how it was hard for his wife to watch all her other friends have kids while she did not have any. When I heard him say that, I instantly thought about how many unnecessary fights are probably caused in marriages today because couples compare themselves to other couples. I believe that it is important for

partners to make a plan for their individual family and stick to it. Otherwise, a couple may always be trying to "keep up with the Joneses." We must realize that every person on earth is different; therefore every couple will be different. Comparing your relationship to other relationships is a sure way to disturb the peace in a home.

9. *Create A Safe House.* My good friends Blake and Stephanie Booth once told me that their marriage is so happy and peaceful because they have created a "Safe House" for one another. They explained that they both understand that neither one of them is perfect, but that they always wanted to be perfectly honest with each other. Blake and Stephanie admitted that sometimes they have thoughts or do things that they should not do as married people. They told me that they have a relationship where they can openly come to one another and confess where they have failed their partner. This helps them to keep peace in their home, because they both don't have to worry about bad news coming from someone else. They know that they can and will, willingly share their faults to make sure nothing comes between them. They have an agreement to love each other past their faults and their short comings, and I believe that is what a lot of marriages are missing these days. They are committed to fighting for each other until the very end. If you don't have a "safe house agreement" with your partner I encourage you to establish one today!

10. *Being Honorable*: I entitled this particular lesson as "Being Honorable" in respect to my good friend and business mentor, Stephen Rowland. Stephen is well known for conquering the world many times over with his massive construction projects. I met Stephen shortly after I was divorced, and gravitated to him because of his quiet confidence, business sense and genuine love for God. After several encounters of being around Stephen I came to find out that Stephen himself had also gone through a divorce many years before mine. His situation was a bit different than mine due to the fact that he had a child involved in the divorce process.

*In the beginning Stephen had a child with the woman he was dating at that current time.* Since he is a humble and respectable man who takes care of his responsibilities, Stephen came to the conclusion that the most honorable thing to do in this situation would be to marry this woman. He admitted to me that it was a mistake on his part, because the chemistry wasn't there between him and his wife at that time. Eventually after several years of trying to force his marriage to work out for the sake of his children, Stephen and his now ex-wife decided to call it quits. Stephen advises that couples that have had an unexpected child should NOT get married unless there is a loving, healthy foundation laid down first. If there is not a natural, loving chemistry between those two partners then the children are being done a disservice. Those children may not have the opportunity to see the way parents are supposed to properly love one another. In return those children may easily grow up to mimic the awkward and unbalanced relationship they witnessed their parents display.

During my time in California, I met an extraordinary individual by the name of Steve Davis. If you ever get the opportunity to meet Steve, your life will instantly be better. He is one of the most positive and encouraging people you will ever encounter in your life. Steve is also built like a bodybuilder, and is one of the strongest men I know physically. I'm sure Steve can easily bench-press over 350 pounds while beating a person in a chess game at the same time! However, what I didn't know is that Steve is also one of the strongest men I would ever meet emotionally. At the current moment when I met Steve, he had a beautiful wife and a great business that was taking off. When I got to know Steve on a more personal level, I came to find out that he had actually been divorced three times previous to his present wife. When he shared this information with me, I legitimately marveled at his inner strength. This man had been through three divorces, and I was ready to call it quits on love after just one. I felt ashamed of myself. If he can keep a positive attitude, then I should be able to as well, and I should pull strength from the wisdom he gained from his marital mistakes.

Steve has been a big brother and an open book to me over the years, and I have learned so many great lessons about life and marriage from his experiences.

A couple of key lessons I learned from Steve are as follows:

1.  *Find familiar frequencies.* Steve taught me about the importance of matching your mate's frequency. He talked about how everyone gives off energy, and some of it is good and some is bad. He brought up how sometimes you can be next to someone who isn't saying anything, but you are getting bad vibes from them. That is someone's frequency. It is equally important to match a person's frequency when looking for a mate. If you are a positive and active person, the last thing you want to do is be tied to someone who is always negative and lazy. Steve blames this for the destruction of one of his divorces. He mentioned how everything in his life was amazing, but he connected with a woman who was emotionally bankrupt. Steve figured that his life was so great that he could pull her up too, but after years of trying, she managed to pull him down to where she was. Friends, please remember that it is so much easier for someone to pull you down than for you to pull someone up. The scary part is, sometimes those people don't even mean to pull you down. They just naturally do. It's one thing to find someone with the same frequency as yours, but it's another thing to maintain that healthy and happy frequency that you and your partner have established. I believe that the best way to maintain a consistent frequency with your mate is by consistently speaking each other's "love language". If you have never heard of the book ***The 5 Love Languages*** by Gary Chapman, I would strongly suggest you pick that up immediately. To make a long and amazing story short, Chapman spells out how every person has a way they like to be loved, with some of those languages consisting of touch, gifts or words of affirmation. This book will help couples determine what their individual love languages are so that they can speak to those partner's needs on a daily basis. Find a mate with a familiar frequency and love them through their love language in order to keep that frequency balanced!

2. *Love unconditionally.* Steve and my good friend Wayne T. explained to me that the world is afraid to love unconditionally. He said, "Anything less than unconditional love will not fuel a successful marriage. People have to be willing to give it all, or don't give anything at all. People can only give their all if they are emotionally healthy. There are a lot of empty people looking for someone else to fill them up. They are looking for someone else to be their joy—someone else to be their peace and make them happy." Friends, no human can really be all that for anyone else. That is already a combination for chaos. One person will drain the other, and then there will be two empty, bitter people. Be happy first, and then both partners can equally feed off one another's positive energy. Love long, love hard, and love unconditionally. It will pay off in the end.

3. *Don't force it.* One of the greatest lessons I've learned from Steve is having enough faith to not force it. He mentioned that his present marriage is a dream come true because they did not force it. He told me that his three divorces happened because, in one way or another, he forced them to happen. With his current wife, he said they didn't even try to impress each other. When they first met, they were both in amazing places in their life, and they simply did not need each other at all. Steve mentioned how their frequencies matched perfectly, and that he literally could not have built a better spouse for the lifestyle he has! He said that his current wife is the first person in his life to really show him unconditional love. They completely trust each other, and I think that is beautiful. He said, "She gives me peace of mind because she respects my heart." I couldn't be happier for my friend Steve and his wife Gina. They have been married over two years now and are still going stronger than ever. I wish them long life and eternal love!

There were many other great love lessons that I learned from friends around the world, but these were just some of the most important ones. I hope that these lessons bless your life and give you the patience you need to wait for the right partner, and the strength you need to be courageous enough to try love one more time.

# FOR BETTER OR WORSE

Note: This chapter wasn't originally part of my book, but I feel that it is a vital element of marriage that people need to seriously consider before they exchange vows.

THE YEAR TO date is 2014, and I had already been back on the East Coast for a little while now because of my new job at the firm. Everything was going great except for the fact that the image of my parents' perfect relationship wasn't perfect anymore. A little over a year ago, my mother was diagnosed with Alzheimer's disease. Due to the fact that doctors said her memory will progressively deteriorate over time, she was no longer permitted to do tasks such as cooking, driving, and several other very important responsibilities that would allow her to be independent. Along with her mind/memory slipping away, her health has also been on the decline at a simultaneous speed. She is no longer able to walk for a long distance or stand on her feet for more than a couple minutes at a time because of pain in her legs and body. At this point, she cannot do much but sleep and eat, which is causing her to gain weight at a rapid rate. She has also become less able to take care of herself as far as bathing and dressing.

At this point, our family figured that things couldn't get any worse, but then they did. On August 16, 2014, as I was sitting at the kitchen table holding my mother's hand, she had a stroke.

Words can't even describe the feeling of pain that came over me when I witnessed the rock in my life crumbling right before my very own eyes. My sister came over immediately and heard my mother's speech slurring and instantly started crying and said, "Why is she talking like this?" A quick executive decision was made for us to take her to the ER and stay with her overnight as doctors ran tests.

The doctor revealed that my mother did in fact have a stroke, but the surprising part was that somehow, this was actually her second stroke. The first one was a long time before that, but our family never knew. My mother was prescribed a laundry list of new medicines to take and was forced into rehabilitation for her body and speech. We visited her every day in rehab, and it seemed to be working as far as getting her speech back up to speed. Once she got home, all the progress that was made was lost because it was hard for my father to keep up with all the new routines, especially since he himself was twelve years older than my mother. At this point, my father now did all the laundry, cooking, cleaning, rehabilitation exercises, medicine distribution, bathing and dressing of my mother, along with anything else you could possibly think of.

When I was a young boy, my father sat me on his lap and was trying to teach me about the depth of God's love. He explained that God's strength is made perfect in our weakness. He told me that if I'm at 50 percent, God will become that other 50 percent needed to be a perfect 100 percent. But if you're at 30 percent, he will be that 70 percent to make you a perfect whole 100 percent. Even if you are at 0 percent, God will become that entire 100 percent you need to be complete. He told me that God will protect and provide for his children, and we must do that for one another.

My entire life, I have watched my parents perfectly and equally bring 50 percent to our family table in every way. I have now witnessed my mother digress to 10 percent, and my father cheerfully and bravely became the entire 90 percent. I believe that if I could just be 10 percent of the man my father is, then I will be 100 percent better than any other man of my generation.

I say all this to say that my parents clearly meant their vows when they said them about forty years ago. There have been times during my parents' marriage where my dad was out of work and my mother would pick up two jobs to make sure the family made it. It is only right and honorable that my father does the same in this situation.

To protect, provide, cherish, and love for better or worse is what my father vowed to do, and he is being a man of his word! My father taught me that all a man really has in this world is his word, and if your word is no good, then you are no good. Dad taught me that God is his word, which is why we can have peace when he says that he will do something, because God cannot lie. That's why when I caught my wife in repeated lies, it hurt so badly. I didn't know who she was after a while because her words and who she was were completely different. To me, trust and loyalty are everything, and if I can't trust someone's word, then I don't even want to be that person's friend, and definitely don't want to be married to them. Every time I caught Sara in a lie, I felt like I found another crack in our foundation to the house and dreams we were trying to build.

My father was with my mother in her prime—when she had the body and face of an African goddess and when she was smart enough to graduate at the top of her nursing class. He was with her when she was strong enough to work two jobs while being pregnant with me, taking college courses and still raising three other children. And now my father is still with my mother when she can't even dress or bathe herself. My father, Edward J. Cavalli., is a *man's man*, and he sticks by his wife and his word for better or worse!

I can't even begin to imagine the pain in my father's heart with this situation. I know he doesn't mind taking care of my mother, but it's just painful to watch him have to watch her deteriorate. I think about all that they have been through together. From making it out of the villages and the diamond mines of Africa, to beating every odd possible and having a successful life in America with no support from anyone. I think about how they managed to have four children and be able to send them through college, to now becoming grandparents together. It breaks my heart to see them conquer the world and then have my mother forget the journey of how they got to the top. I tear up even as I write this because it really is sad. I never thought I would see my queen like this. I didn't take this into consideration when I fell in love with her in my youngest youth.

My siblings and I do our best to come to my parents' home every weekend and relieve some of the pressure off my father because he is also very tired. I spend many days telling my mom the same old jokes over and over just like the movie *50 First Dates* because she forgets the jokes after I say them, but she remembers that she loves to laugh. I help bathe her when possible and help her do her makeup when my sisters aren't around, before we go to church, because she tells me she still wants to look beautiful for my dad. I'll even spend some nights just holding her while she lies in bed and singing to help her fall asleep quicker. When it's just me and her, she cries sometimes because she feels bad that some of her health choices in life have put her in this situation to be such a burden on my father and family. I tell her that it is okay and that no one is mad at her. I try to help her understand that it's not her fault. Its funny that out of all the things she forgets she reminds me of a promise I made to her when I was 9 years old. I promised her that I would introduce her to Oprah some day,so when she sees me she will say, "I still haven't met Oprah yet." Then I laugh and plead for her to give me a little more time to make it happen.

On those Saturday nights when I travel to spend time with her, she argues with me to go out and enjoy my life, but, she is my life. I don't care about chasing girls any more or trying to be the toughest in the streets. I just care about making the rest of her life the best of her life. If that takes coming every Saturday night and telling her jokes until 2056, then so be it. She came to America with my father to pursue happiness, and I just want to give that to her. It's just crazy to me how quickly life can change—for the better or for the worst. I just know that if I ever get married again, I'll be ready for either.

Lesson: Gentlemen, don't make vows that you don't plan to keep. Consider the best *and* the worst scenarios if you are going to make a vow to someone. My father never could have imagined his beautiful, strong, vibrant bride would end up like this. Ladies, please do *not* accept vows from a man who you don't believe would take care of you in the worst-case situation. If you cannot honestly say that the man you are with would take care of you the way my father does for my mother, then you quite possibly may be with the wrong man. Just know that you are worth it! I've heard countless stories of women getting in an accident and the husband leaving for another woman and vice versa. Please do not be in a rush, ladies and gents. You are worth the wait and worth being cared for!

# MY SINCEREST APOLOGIES

THERE IS OBVIOUSLY no easy part to getting or being divorced, but I will say that one of the absolute worst parts of it is all the people that get hurt in the process. I wasn't aware how many innocent bystanders got impacted by this bomb of bad news until the smoke cleared, and I actually started counting bodies. I have heard of divorces between couples that ended peacefully, but ours ended horribly, and I'm a big part to blame for that. About a year after the divorce was finally finalized, I remember getting a call from Sara while I was driving my car. She was expressing how everything just felt different in the worst way. She told me how our divorce really shook up the church and how badly people were hurt by "our" decision to get the divorce. She told me how all her siblings were disgusted with me and how they were scared to get married now. She told me that she wished I would have fought harder for her because now all her friends thought that men would just easily quit on them. I know I personally fought as hard as I sensibly could have without going crazy, but I guess to our little world of friends and family, it looked like I just woke up and gave up one random day. She explained to me how hard it was for her to not cry when the kids from her Sunday school class would still mistakenly call her Mrs. Cavalli. Sara said that half of her class time was spent helping the children understand why she was not Mrs. Cavalli anymore. She said the kids just don't get it, and she really didn't either. I knew the answer to that brain-dead question, but I wanted to keep peace with her on the phone since it had been the longest time I've gone without talking to her since I met her. In my head, I said, *"it's because you're a crazy, bipolar, compulsive liar."* As Sara was going down the list of people we have hurt and confused, my heart just sank further and further into my stomach.

I could hear Sara's voice getting weaker on the phone as she began to go deeper into detail. She began to tell me how hard it was for her to explain to her little cousins, who were the flower girls in our wedding, that Leonardo was never coming back. Sara told me how they just kept asking if I was going away on another long business trip. She told me how stern she had to be with them and how she finally broke down one day and accidently yelled at them, saying, "He is never ever coming back, okay? No more piggyback rides, no more shoulder helicopter spins, no more movie dates, no more dancing in the rain, no more hide-and-seek, no more bedtime stories, no more guitar and singing lessons from him . . . No more anything from Leonardo . . . *ever*!" As Sara kept screaming and crying in the phone, all I could do was pull over, drop the phone on my lap, put my hands over my face, lean back in my seat and reflect in pain. I would never want to hurt those little girls or the children from her church class. I would never want to hurt her family or the people in her church regardless of how bad they treated me during the divorce. Hearing this news from her just made me feel like the scum of the earth. It was no longer me falling out of love with Sara but falling out of love with over nine hundred people at the same time. As if losing your wife wasn't hard enough, it is also losing tons of people I considered my new family from her two churches. I lost friends, colleagues, and mentors all in one clean swoop. She told me how so many people from her churches were praying that we got back together. Like most men, I'm a problem solver, and I want to fix problems; so for a quick second, I almost tried to figure out a way for us to make it work again. Then I instantly remembered how much of a liar and faking snake she was, and how I would literally rather burn to death than live under the oppression of her fraudulent father. I knew what she was saying was the truth though because I was being privately messaged from people in her church, asking if I was okay and if they thought that Sara and I were ever getting back together again. I always tried to respond back as politically correct as possible because even though I couldn't stand Sara and her family, I didn't ever want to cause disruption in a church congregation.

I know that I personally hurt a lot of people, so I wanted take this piece of my book and say that I, Leonardo Cavalli, am sorry.

To my ex's church congregations: I first wanted to thank everyone from that church who stood by me during and after the divorce. You know exactly who you are. I appreciated every single encouraging word you ever spoke into my life during that depressing, dark time. I wish you all the best, and I hope that there will be someone to come to your aid the same way you came to mine when I wanted to give up. I know how many of you used Sara and my relationship when things were good as an example to your children of how to do things the "right way". I feel like I let everyone down. I wish I could have been a better role model in that area for your children. It still bothers me about how messy everything fell apart, and for that, I would like to say I'm sorry.

To the children of my ex's church: You may still be too young to understand this now, but when you are older, I hope that this book finds its way into your hands and its message finds its way into your heart. Take your time to find love, and if you are fortunate enough to find it, do not let it go. Keep it BAMN (by any means necessary). Just know that I still love you all. I wish that I got the chance to properly say good-bye to all of you, and because I did not, I wanted to say I'm sorry.

To my flower-power girls: From the day I met you little angels, I was told that you would be the flower girls in my wedding! I'm glad that we got to make that dream come true, but I just wish that we were able to keep the dream alive. What happened between Sara and I had nothing to do with you all. I miss spending time with all of you little divas. I hope that my divorce doesn't scare you from falling in love someday. Love and life are still beautiful—you just have to do both with the right people. I know I left you with many unanswered questions and a handful of heartbreaks, and for that, I am sorry.

To my best man: I hate that our friendship ended the way it did. I hope that one day you will understand that I just wanted us to live an honest life, not a perfect life. I'm proud that you finally did the right thing and told your girlfriend. I am also glad that your stars eventually aligned, and you got to marry the girl of your dreams with a clear conscience. I wish blessings over you and your growing family. If I've never said it before, then I want you to know that I'm proud of you and I still love you bro. I'm sorry.

To my parents: Dad and Mom, I can't say I that I'm sorry enough to the both of you. Thank you for all that you have done for me and our family, and I apologize about the shame I have brought on our family through this divorce. I should have realized that the parents that had me also instinctively had my best interest at heart. I know that in your heart it hurt you to not to be at my wedding, but I wanted to let you know that I forgive both of you for not being there. I still don't agree with the way it was done, but I truly forgive you for it. I'm sorry for distancing myself from the family for two years, especially when it was some of the most difficult times for our family. I'm sorry for all the arguments and the fights we had since Sara came into my life. I will make sure to get your blessings next time around. I'm sorry for delaying your Cavalli grandchildren. Give me another five years, and keep praying that I find a girl who isn't crazy ;-)

To my future wife: If you're still out there, I just wanted to say that I am so sorry for everything. I say *if* because I hope my actions have not detoured me in life beyond the point of return to the place I've never been, which is with you. I'm so sorry. I'm sorry for being overambitious and settling for a woman who couldn't have been more wrong for me. I'm sorry for all the women I've been with, trying to fill a hole that you'll be able to seal with ease. I'm so sorry for the baggage I've acquired over these past couple years. However, I can assure you that all the fires and storms I have been through were not in vain. I am the best version of me that I could ever be at this point in my life. I think about where you could be every day, and I look forward to meeting you. Please accept my apologies as they are the sincerest.

NOTE: I will be re-releasing this book around a year from now, but I want to hear all of the life lessons that my readers have learned through their relationships as well. I am only one man and I do not know it all, nor have I been through it all. I need your help and your wisdom to save various generations from making the same mistakes that we have made. Please help me by going to my website and leaving a comment on my blog, or emailing me your story. Thank you in advance for your help!

# FINAL THOUGHTS

IN THESE FINAL thoughts, I wanted to briefly address three of the most frequent questions that I've gotten asked over the past couple years. I will answer them as truthfully as possible. These questions are as follows:

1. Q: Do you think you got divorced because you were too young?
   A: Absolutely not! Young, middle-aged, and elderly people get divorced all the time. There are very immature older couples, and then there are also very mature and responsible younger married couples. Now, people who get married at an older age than twenty-four may have a higher ratio for staying together, but there really is no perfect magical number for getting married. My friends Dave and Britney Fox, whom I have known for ten years, have been married since they were twenty-one years old. Brittany was actually eighteen years old when they tied the knot. I'm proud to say that they recently celebrated their eighth year of marriage. They are a perfect example of a younger couple that is far more mature than many older couples I work with. At this point in their lives, they couldn't be any more successful in their individual careers, and they couldn't be any happier in their marriage!

   Every person is a variable, and every couple is different. I'll be the last person to say that a couple is too young to marry. However, what I will say is, make sure both people in the relationship are happy with themselves and have a good sense of who they are. I say "a good sense of who they are" because I feel that we are always in a state of discovering ourselves. Certain situations we go through in our lives will expose hidden qualities and flaws that we were not aware of. Sometimes those life-altering situations may not come until later in life, or they may happen earlier in life, but I do believe that they always come. When these circumstances do come, I advise you to stand firm on what your foundational beliefs are and not waver like

I did in my darkest hour. I would also advise couples to have steady jobs and living situations before tying the knot. That should be common wisdom when planning a life together, but you would be surprised at what I have heard when speaking with some newly married couples. Lastly, a couple should get married when they are comfortable—not when parents or loved ones force them to. Time is your friend, so use it to show you the truth about certain situations. Time really does tell it all in its own due time.

2.   Q: Females always ask me, "Is the monster inside you gone now?"

A: I can honestly say that the monster created within me during my "dark side" period is gone. During the dark-side period in my life, I would have moments of remorse where I would try and go back to being a good guy. When I would try to turn back into a good guy, girls would try to play games with my heart, so I would go back to being a jerk and sleeping with several other women. After years of going through that destructive cycle, I finally found a girl I thought I was going to possibly marry one day. I'll call this lady Lauren. I met Lauren years after my divorce. Lauren chased me for four months because I just didn't trust any females at this point. When I finally gave her a chance to be my lady, things were going perfectly. Keep in mind that we were doing long distance, and she was (ironically) from Chicago, just like Sara. We visited each other every month, just like I did with Sara. Lauren and I even agreed to similar rules to the ones I agreed to with Sara. Everything was going perfect for four months until I caught Lauren in a lie. This time around, I was going to pay attention to the red flags. I called Lauren out on it and came to find out that Lauren slept with literally all her male friends before I met her. If that wasn't embarrassing enough, she was also still hanging out with one of them while I was in a relationship with her. As mentioned before, Lauren and I agreed not to spend alone time with people we had been dating. After hearing this information, I weighed out all the options I had. The next day, I told her that I couldn't be with someone who would lie to my face about doing things behind my back. Now in my dark period, this is the point where I would snap back into monster mode, but this time around, I realized that I didn't have to go down that route anymore. I just went back to being single old me. I decided to never let anyone have control over my feelings or how I reacted again. I was a new man and decided to take the high road whenever I was faced with a situation like that. I am proud to say that the monster is gone! Friends, please remember that even though hurt people hurt other people, hurting people won't heal you.

The saddest part about that situation with Lauren was how bad the break up hurt my dad. My dad was already calling this lady my future fiancé, but he didn't even meet her yet. She was actually supposed to meet my parents the following week, right before I broke things off with her. I think my dad honestly took the break up harder than I did, because I believe he was hurting for me. He had already seen me go through so much with the divorce that I guess he just finally wanted to see things work out in the favor of his son. I also knew that he really wanted grandsons from me because none of his grandchildren have the Cavalli last name yet. Hopefully next time I'll get it right for us dad.

3. Q: What do you predict the future of marriage will be like?
A: To be honest, I'm quite fearful for the future of marriage. So many changes have already happened in the last five years that I believe its true meaning was lost in translation over time. What I am truly fearful of is the fact that if divorce rates keep skyrocketing like they have been year after year already, then one day I may have to give seminars to children on the ancient concept of marriage. I fear that one day, which may not be too far away from now, I will have to explain that once upon a time, there was a thing where a man and woman who loved each other, made vows to one another and created children. Then that couple that made those children stayed together, for the rest of their natural lives. That thought breaks my heart. I hope the world never gets to that point, but at the rate society is going right now, it seems that conclusion would be the only feasible outcome. I feel that we are in the fast lane to destruction,

and there are currently no roadblocks in place to stop it from happening. I hope that this book helps reverse some of the effects of popular culture, with people in Hollywood getting divorced every three years like it's the "cool thing to do". I hate that people treat marrying their partner like leasing a car, and that when a person gets "bored" with them, they trade them in for a newer model. I'm optimistic that this book will do what it was originally intended to do, which is save marriages and stop faulty marriages from even taking place.

SINCE THESE ARE my final thoughts, I want to say that I appreciate everyone who took time to purchase and read this book. I hope that this book has blessed your life in one way or another. If it has, I would like to ask you to pass it along to someone else who may need it more than you. I have exposed all my good, bad, and ugly in hopes that no one else would fall into the same ditches that I did. I am declaring an all-out war against divorce, and I would like you to join with me. Please go to my website, www.24andDivorced.com. and give testimonials about how this book has impacted your life if it has. I am always open to collaborating with like-minded, positive people. My dream is to get this book into every college, every library, every bookstore, every church, every marriage counselor's office, and every courting/engaged/ married couple's hands! I just want to see people fall in love and stay in love for life! Thank you for your time.

Your friend,
Leonardo Cavalli

Contact information for Mr. Cavalli:

Used for bookings/ guest appearances/ tour and  music updates

www.24andDivorced.com
My Email: 24andDivorced@gmail.com
My Office: (612) 747-7782
Facebook: Leonardo Cavalli
Insta Gram: @King_Cavalli
Twitter: @King_Cavalli
www.BandCamp.com: King Cavalli
SoundCloud.com: King Cavalli
ReverbNation.com: King Cavalli
WhatsApp: (612)747-7782 Leonardo Cavalli

# SONGS FROM THE CITY OF SORROW
## (MY HEART)

All songs are available and free to download at
www.24andDivorced.com

These songs are written and song by myself, but produced by mega-producer PARKER!

Please visit my website the last week of every month to stay updated on all my newly released music and bonus footage!

Enjoy ☺


## AFRAID:

**I'm Afraid**

**VERSE 1:**
**Drinks are pouring / Money throwing in the air**
**Lights are flashing / Women dancing everywhere**
**In this crowd of people I'm all by myself**
**And of all the fears I evade I'm not afraid to say I'm afraid . . .**

**That I just might fall, like the money from the sky, oh why am I so afraid of.**
**That I might want more, of the drinks they pour, oh lord I'm so afraid of.**

**The women, so tempting, I might start sinning again,**

**I'm so afraid of . . . I'm so afraid of me now.**

CHORUS:
And I'm AFRAIIIIIIID (2x)
I'm so afraid of me now

Verse 2:
I fear I'll get the call, that tells me she won't wait.
I'll rush to be with her, but she'll say I'm too late
I fear my heart turns cold, so cold that it will break
I fear I'll find true love, then find out it was fake
-I'm afraid I turned to drugs, I'm afraid I might abuse
-Can't give my heart away, to easily I bruise
- I've been through the same girls, I swear it's deja vu
-I'm afraid I'll never find a girl that I'm afraid to lose

PRE-CHORUS:

That I just might fall, like the money from the sky, oh why am I
so afraid of.
That I might want more, of the drinks they pour, oh lord I'm so
afraid of.

The women, so tempting, I might start sinning again,
I'm so afraid of . . . I'm so afraid of me now.

CHORUS:
And I'm AFRAAAAAID (2x)

I'm so afraid of me now

And I'm Not afraid to say that I'm afraid
And of all the fears I evade I'm not afraid to say I'm afraid

And I'm Not afraid to say that I'm afraid
And of all the fears I evade I'm not afraid to say I'm afraid

And I'm Not afraid to say that I'm afraid
And of all the fears I evade I'm not afraid to say I'm afraid

# I CARE FOR YOU

CHORUS:
I'd give my air for you, to prove that I cared for you
Burdens I bare for you, cause I really care for you

VERSE 1:
I really cared, and I'm still here
Right where you left me when you disappeared
And after all you put me through, I would still give my life for you
My family shed a few tears, we didn't speak for two years
Got married in November, went crazy by the New Years
I moved half way around the country, just to make you happy
Who knew that in six months, in half you would snap me
You ran game so fast you lapped me
In all your little lies you trapped me
If I gave you a gun you might load it up and cap me
I'd give up my Maybach to help you find your way back, to me. I hope one day you'll see that . . .

Chorus:
I'd give my air for you, to prove that I cared for you
Burdens I bare for you, cause I really care for you

VERSE 2:
And you can't say I wasn't there for you with all the things I was prepared to do
Girl you broke my heart. I guess I wasn't prepared for you
I would give my last breath just so you could live.
I'd give you my all, give a rib up for my rib
If I was broke I'd rob a bank just to make sure that you eat
If someone disrespects you just know we're going to bang out in the street.
I go so hard for our love, cause without you I'm incomplete
Girl I would fall into the sun if it'd protect you from the heat, cause.

Chorus:
I'd give my air for you, to prove that I cared for you
Burdens I bare for you, cause I really care for you

# LIE TO ME

VERSE 1:
I know lately things haven't been the best
But I need to get something off my chest
You're moving out, and it's making me depressed
Love don't live here, and this needs to be addressed

PRE-CHORUS
So baby let's talk about it, you got your bags and you walking out
But you still got my heart girl, and how am I to live without it
And now my hearts full of sorrow, I'll face the truth tomorrow . . .
But for now, please lie to me

CHORUS:
Tell me I'm the one that you can't wait to see
Tell me in my arms is where you want to be
I don't ask for much, this is my only plea
So can you, lie to me / I need you to, lie to me / Baby will you, lie to me

VERSE 2:
I can tell that there's somebody else
But I can't see myself with nobody else
If I could freeze time I'd keep things the same
Cause you know that I'm not good with change

PRE-CHORUS
So baby let's talk about it, you got your bags and you walking out
But you still got my heart girl, and how am I to live without it
And now my hearts full of sorrow, I'll face the truth tomorrow . . .
But for now, please lie to me

CHORUS:
Tell me I'm the one that you can't wait to see
Tell me in my arms is where you want to be
I don't ask for much, this is my only plea
So can you, lie to me / I need you to, lie to me / Baby will you, lie to me

Printed in the United States
By Bookmasters